FUNERALS
WITH TODAY'S
FAMILIES *in* MIND

FUNERALS
WITH TODAY'S
FAMILIES *in* MIND

A Handbook for Pastors

Doreen M. McFarlane

THE
PILGRIM
PRESS
Cleveland

*I dedicate this book
to the memory of the many dear people
whose funerals and memorial services
I have conducted over the years.
May they rest in peace and find themselves
in the glorious company of the saints.
And may their families continue to go on,
in courage, trust, and faith.*

The Pilgrim Press
700 Prospect Avenue
Cleveland, Ohio 44115-1100
thepilgrimpress.com

© 2008 by Doreen M. McFarlane

❀ Printed in the United States of America on acid-free paper that contains post-consumer fiber.

12 11 10 09 08   5 4 3 2 1

Library of Congress Cataloging-in-Publication Data
McFarlane, Doreen M.
    Funerals with today's families in mind : a resource for pastors / by
Doreen M. McFarlane.
        p. cm.
    ISBN-13: 978-0-8298-1786-7 (alk. paper)
    1. Church work with the bereaved. 2. Funeral rites and ceremonies.
I. Title.
BV4330.M34 2008
264'.85 – dc22

2007040167

contents

part three
special circumstances

part four
funeral sermons

part five
funeral resources at your church

preface

Funerals are a fact of life in the ministry of every pastor. We never know when we will be called to officiate at one, and they have a way of coming up during the busiest times. I have written this book to offer practical comments, tips, and suggestions. I also present theological reflections that relate to the various aspects of funeral ministry. In addition, I offer a variety of short funeral stories called "scenarios," interspersed throughout the book, which I hope will offer examples and inspiration.

The idea for this book came to me when I was about three-quarters through writing my recent wedding book, *Weddings with Today's Families in Mind: A Handbook for Pastors*. The two books are intended as companion volumes, offering practical information that relates directly to your daily work as a pastor. It is my great hope that you will find both of these books useful for your own pastoral library.

I would like to thank The Pilgrim Press, Timothy Staveteig, Kim Martin Sadler, John Eagleson, and Ulrike Guthrie for their editorial work.

I am grateful also to my husband, Michael, for his devoted support of my writing, teaching, and ministry, and to our daughters and their families who bring such joy to our lives.

FUNERALS
WITH TODAY'S
FAMILIES *in* MIND

introduction

■ why this book?

All of us pastors, whether we are senior pastors, associates, or assistants, are likely to be called upon quite often to officiate at funerals and memorial services.* Yet we are often ill prepared for the practical aspects of this work. Though most of us have learned to get by, few of us have the time or information to hone our funeral ministry skills. Many pastors go through years of ministry feeling more than a bit uncomfortable every time they are asked to lead a funeral service.

■ family members need special attention

The call to officiate at a funeral service will come from the funeral home or directly from a family member of the deceased. The deceased may be a member of your church, an acquaintance, or on occasion, even a total stranger. Losing a loved one is incredibly difficult for families, whether or not they are churchgoers. Your careful attention to detail and your professional and caring pastoral leadership will mean more to these individuals and families than you will ever know. Not only at times of great joy (such as weddings) but also in times of crisis and death we pastors are afforded the opportunities to bond with families in our churches, as well as people in the larger community. Our actual contact time with family members of the deceased is often short, but the experiences we share are intense and likely to become deeply engrained in memories.

---

*Throughout the book, when I use the word "funeral," it will also include memorial services. Memorial services are, of course, services in honor of the deceased at which no body and usually no ashes are present.

The particular focus of this book is the families and ways we can best meet their needs. Today's families come in all configurations. Many have experienced divorce and remarriage, sometimes more than once or in more than one generation. Many more than in previous generations are the products of intermarriage among religions and cultures. There are more openly gay and lesbian marriages and partnerships, often with children. And, of course, various configurations of people are now living together as loving families in this new century, some without the official bond of marriage. Love knows no bounds and, when there is a death in a family, mourners come in all sexes, ages, religions, and cultures. When we Christian pastors are asked to lead a funeral service, we need to be ready to serve all of these grieving loved ones with both expertise and sincerity.

■ you, the pastor, as facilitator

In preparing for and officiating at any funeral or memorial service, a wide variety of your pastoral skills will come into play. These include your gifts for administration, preaching, pastoral care, and hospitality. Though you will very likely be more talented in some of these areas than others, this is no reason why you cannot do a superb job at leading the family in a healing and meaningful experience and a hope-giving service. Every service that you have the honor and opportunity to lead affords you one more chance to hone your skills and extend God's loving compassion. So do not be discouraged if you have not yet performed the perfect funeral service. All of us are works in process. Know what your best gifts are and use them. But also be aware of your weakest points, and be intentional about working to improve them. It won't be long before you feel quite comfortable with all the aspects of this important component of your ministry.

Whether you are new to the ministry or an old hand looking for ideas or for confirmation of what you are already doing, in this book I will guide you through each step, from your first meeting with the family, through the wake, the day of the service at the church or funeral home, and then also to the cemetery or memorial garden, as well as the reception. We will consider all kinds of special circumstances that crop up at funerals and take a look at some sample sermons. I offer guidance on starting up and caring for a memorial garden, as well as on how to prepare a brochure on death and dying that suits your particular congregation.

Funerals rarely fit easily into a pastor's schedule. The book is designed for you to grab it from your shelf to look up chapters that address specific problems you are facing right now. But why not also make some time in your schedule and read this little book all the way through so you know what's there when you need it? My hope is that, having done that, you'll be ready for almost any funeral.

part one

preparation for the funeral or memorial service

I

 ## meeting with the bereaved to gather family information

■ the deceased person's relationships with the immediate family

At the outset, find out which individual is the closest family member of the deceased. In the case of a married person, it will likely be the spouse. With an elderly person predeceased by the spouse, it will likely be the person's children equally. The family may choose one person to be their representative and your main contact. This is often the eldest. If there are no children, it will probably be a sibling of the deceased, but it could be any family member. If there is no family, it may even be a friend. If it is the funeral home that contacted you, then your primary contact will have been determined by them. So if someone calls or arrives at your office to ask you to officiate at a service, do make absolutely sure you are speaking with the "primary" contact, the one officially responsible for making decisions about the service.

When the primary contact is the spouse, there are times when this person will be in so much grief that decision making will be difficult or even impossible. This could, of course, also be the case if the contact is a parent, a beloved sibling, or even a friend. You will have to determine if the person seems to be making reasonable choices. If not, then you might get the rest of the immediate family to meet with you, along with the primary person, so choices can be made together about the funeral. It is important, however, that — even if you do get the gathered group to agree on a decision — the primary person also agrees and is not being coerced by the rest of the family.

■ getting needed information about the rest of the family

You will need a list of the names and relationships to the deceased. If the closest family member is not in a state of mind to give this information accurately, you can usually get it from the obituary although it may be a day or so before you have it in your hands. The funeral home can usually provide this.

Once you have the list of names of family members it is a good idea to ask: "Is there anyone else whose name you have not mentioned?" Many families have a parent, a sister, brother, child, or grandchild who is estranged. The person giving you the list may be intentionally or unintentionally leaving a name out, expecting that this person will not show up at the service. Still, should they turn up and find their name left out, there could be hurt feelings or bigger problems. If the one who engaged you to perform the service specifically asks you not to speak the name of this estranged person, then you may need to comply. Still, it is better to include the name if you can. Estranged or not, the person is still a part of the family.

While you have the family or contact person in your office, ask if they are expecting any special guests — perhaps people who will have traveled long distances, dignitaries, or members of the armed forces. That way you will be able to make arrangements for their seating.

■ the choices and the non-negotiables for the service

The closest loved one, often along with family members, will have some decisions to make regarding the service itself. What these choices are will be up to you. They may include the following:

+ Will there be a bulletin printed?

+ Will there be a eulogy that is separate from the meditation/sermon or will it be included in that context? This usually depends on who is giving the eulogy.

+ What scripture passages and/or poetry readings will be chosen and who will read them?

+ Will there be hymns sung by the congregation? What hymns? What, if any, other music will be performed, and by whom?

+ If the person is not being cremated and the body is present at the service, will the service be with an open casket or closed casket? Whether this is negotiable usually depends on the traditions of your denomination, local church, community, and the personal choice of the family. (You might also consider whether you and any readers or musical soloists are comfortable doing a service with the open casket up there with you.)

■ about the fees

The best time to inform the family about fees related to the service is usually toward the end of your first meeting to gather family information. Though you usually have to do this yourself, it is better if someone like a church secretary can put together some kind of official card with these fees clearly listed (fees having been agreed upon by the appropriate decision-making body of your church) and give this to the family or representative. The card will include the cost for your services as pastor, for the church organist and any related soloists, a custodial fee, and sometimes a fee for church use. Will you be charging for printed bulletins? And how about a fee or donation request for whatever church group is taking responsibility for putting on any meal or reception in the church hall following the service? Whose responsibility is the flowers? (Typically it is the family's responsibility to order these, but some churches have other customs.)

In most churches, the costs for some of the above services may differ, depending on whether the deceased (or, sometimes, a family member of the deceased) is a church member. The difference in fees is not intended to discriminate against non–church members but to acknowledge that a funeral service is one of the privileges of church membership.

It is sometimes possible for your church secretary to be the one who hands the fee card to the family, either when they come in to meet with you or when they are leaving, and politely tells them how and when the fees should be paid. A common way to make the payment is for the family to provide envelopes with cash or checks in advance of the day of the service. These can be given to you, the secretary, or a deacon, who will then disperse them discreetly. Why should this be done in advance of the day of the service? First, because the family is very likely to be distracted the day of the service and can understandably forget to bring or distribute the funds. Second, because any outsiders such as guest organists or other soloists ought to receive their pay before leaving the church; better yet, out of respect, they should be paid before they make the music. Third, because you do not want to have the embarrassing task of asking for money after the day of the service.

If you are doing a service at the funeral home, the funeral directors will negotiate your fee with you in advance, and this will be part of the family's overall payment to the funeral home. The funeral home will give you a check. If they do not mention the fee when they request that you perform a service, it is perfectly appropriate for you to ask, or simply tell them what fee you expect to receive.

■ the previous pastor, your predecessor

It is common in times of a death for family members to long for the pastoral care of a favorite or longtime minister. This minister is not always you, simply because the previous minister may have baptized them, married them, or brought them into the church when they became members. Sometimes the previous pastor has become a close friend of their family. Still, you are the pastor now, and it should be you who performs the service. There are many reasons for this. Most important, it is at times of crisis that pastor and people have the best chance to bond. Second, the retired pastor is just that — retired. The pastor who has left for another church has moved on. With a gentle explanation from you, families usually understand and they will welcome your ministry to them. Once the day of the service has passed, it is likely to be you that they will be asking for — yes, even after you retire! Then it will be your turn to decline.

2

 decisions at the funeral home

■ your involvement or lack of involvement

As pastor, it is unlikely that you will be involved in the decisions the family members make at the funeral home, but it is possible that the family will ask you for advice. If the family invites you to accompany them on their initial visit to the funeral home, they may want you to help them with the decisions they will be asked to make. If you do go to the funeral home with them, it is important that you don't interfere and that you say as little as possible. The decisions are very personal and are ultimately theirs. The only time you might speak up would be if you sense that grieving family members don't understand the decisions they are being expected to make, or if the primary decision-making person appears to misunderstand information that you heard clearly.

■ the cost of a service

The expenses for the service will vary greatly from state to state. Educate yourself in advance about what might be a reasonable cost for a simple service, a mid-priced service, and a higher level of service. You are unlikely to know the financial situation of the bereaved, so it is best to stay silent, unless you feel you are truly needed or they ask for information or advice. Your presence in supporting and standing with the family will usually be enough.

■ burial or cremation?

Most people will have made it clear to their loved ones, long before the time comes, whether they prefer burial or cremation.

This decision is often made for emotional or theological reasons more than reasons related to family history or even culture. Still, you will encounter situations where the deceased has not expressed a preference and the family may struggle with the decision and may turn to you for advice. For that reason it is good to have considered the possible reasons for each choice.

Burial

Burial is the most traditional Western method. It involves more expense than cremation, mainly because the body will have to be embalmed and a casket purchased. In addition, any transportation of the casket raises the cost of the funeral. Add to that the cost of a burial plot and some kind of headstone or marker. Many cemeteries require the purchase of an additional outer casing for the casket.

Some reasons for choosing burial over cremation include that burial has been the traditional norm of Western society, and therefore of many individual families you encounter. Even though cremation may be much more practical for any number of reasons (some listed above), many people will still choose burial. Some people choose burial for emotional, spiritual, or theological reasons — just as they do for cremation too. Reasons can be deeply emotional and cannot always be easily explained. The most likely reason is that their loved ones who died before have been buried.

Whatever the wishes of the deceased, one hopes they will have been communicated to the family in advance. Family members are usually willing to choose the mode of body disposal that the person has requested. There are some occasions when this is not the case. Sometimes, for example, the spouse or family may really feel uncomfortable with cremation (or with burial). Even if they try to get you to advise them, remember that the decision must be theirs. You can, perhaps, help them keep in mind the wishes of the deceased but, unless the wishes were expressed in writing, the decision of the immediate family will be followed.

Cremation

There are many reasons people choose cremation. Cremation is much less expensive; it is also fast and uncomplicated and can quite easily be arranged and even paid for in advance. Some people have an aversion to the idea of being buried. Others choose cremation for ecological reasons, noting that cemeteries take up space on good land that could otherwise be used for more fruitful pursuits such as agriculture, homes, or parks. Still others choose cremation because they don't care for the idea of a "fuss" being made over them at their demise. They want simply to be cremated and be gone, feeling that this way they will be less trouble for the living.

If cremation is the choice, I always discourage loved ones from taking the ashes home, even for a short period. I suggest that they keep them in my office until the time of scattering or burial. Why? In some cases, even with deeply loved deceased persons, the family member will tuck away the box with the ashes in a closet or some place out of the way and then feel a good deal of guilt about not paying some kind of proper respect. In other cases, after bringing the ashes home, loved ones find it difficult to let go of them when the time comes to scatter them or place them at a chosen site or in a memorial garden.

SCENARIO

George and Selma had been deeply in love. Even though she had had a serious health condition throughout their married life, when she died quite suddenly in her late fifties George was devastated. When the pastor suggested the ashes be kept in his office until the time of their placement in the memorial garden, George understood and agreed. When the ashes were placed in the garden, George noticed that they had come in a brown plastic container. He asked the pastor if he could take the container home and the pastor agreed. Months later George told the pastor that he had placed photos of his beloved Selma inside the plastic box and had kept that box on the table beside his bed. Even though he had not taken the ashes home, George had still found a tangible item to turn into a kind of icon — an item to bring out and look at, through which he could feel some sense of Selma's presence. Over time, he got past this stage of his grief and was able to give up the box and move on.

■ caskets and urns

Purchasing an urn

In most cases, the purchase of an urn is unnecessary. With cremation, if the family does not pay for an urn, they will be given the ashes in a small box, with the ashes inside in a plastic bag, usually closed with a twist tie. The box in some cases is biodegradable cardboard. In other instances, it may be a strong dark plastic box that can be pried open at the top. The name of the deceased will be clearly marked on this box.

The funeral home may or may not encourage the family to purchase an urn. These come in a wide range of styles and prices. Unless the family plans to retain the ashes over a long period of time, they do not need an urn and indeed there are many circumstances in which it cannot be used. In many places, if the ashes are going to be placed in the ground, there are local laws that allow only the loose ashes (and in some cases in a biodegradable container) to be placed into the ground. The reason for this legal ruling is often related to water levels in particular places. In some locations, where there is too much rain, urns and even caskets are in danger of floating back up from the ground during heavy rains. When a family has purchased an urn, the ashes may be in the urn only until the actual placing of the ashes into the ground or the scattering of the ashes. Families then rarely have any use for them, and these urns can become a strange kind of burden: there is no good place to put them. Most families do not want them on the mantelpiece, but they also don't want them hidden in the closet. Spouses and families find it difficult to throw the urns away, even though the ashes are no longer in them.

Purchasing a casket

If the person is to be buried, the loved ones will be asked to purchase a casket. Caskets vary greatly in price and affect the overall funeral fee, which varies mainly according to the choice of the casket. The quality of caskets also varies widely. They come from simple and inexpensive cloth-covered pine caskets all the way to the classic oak caskets with brass handles. Caskets also come in various types of aluminum and steel and with decorations such as floral designs or even photographs of the deceased. There will also be choices with regard to color and materials for the casket's lining and the small pillow placed under the head of the deceased.

Loved ones who are making these decisions, being deeply distressed over the death, sometimes make extravagant choices. If the opportunity arises, it is not inappropriate for you as pastor to make some gentle suggestions, while also assuring the loved ones that the decision is of course theirs. If, for example, you happen to know that the family is not financially flush, you might remind them (if you think it is the case) that their deceased might have wanted them to choose a less extravagant casket, so there would be more money to be used for them to continue their lives. Of course, their decision still depends on factors that you cannot always know.

SCENARIO _____

> Zena had never had money. It was nobody's fault really, but just the circumstances of her life. She had spent most of her life living with her sister Laura. Together they had cared for their mother and later raised Zena's son together without the benefit of a father. Laura had worked for years while Zena had been the one to stay home, cook, keep house, and care for the child. The result was that, from about the age of thirty, Zena had never really had her own money. Still, she did all right and never really wanted for anything.
>
> Over the years Zena had often spoken about what her funeral service would be like. She used to smile just thinking about it. When she departed from this world, she wanted a good

send-off with a Scottish piper in full regalia and, for her body, a fine oak casket. Fortunately, her son had grown to be quite successful in this world. He was happy to provide his mother's two wishes. Zena looked so beautiful in that oak casket, as if she'd been a woman of means all of her life. Hers was one beautiful funeral service and all the family felt good about their decision to fulfill Zena's dream and last wishes.

■ at church, the funeral home, or the gravesite?

Many people of strong faith desire that the funeral or memorial service take place in the sanctuary of the church. Memorial services are easier. Today, having the casket present at the service is becoming less and less popular, probably because of increased costs. Still, funeral homes are certainly able to provide this. In some churches, mainly Orthodox churches, a cloth called a pall is used to cover the casket during the service. Also, there are sometimes regulations or traditions regarding the positioning of the casket in the sanctuary.* These are usually listed in denominational books of worship. Those families who prefer a simple service will often ask the pastor to come and say a few words at the gravesite only.**

■ the wake or visitation

The loved ones may ask you for advice about holding a visitation or wake, and whether you think it is important. Rather than offering your personal opinions, try to find out what their own ideas and family traditions are. Do your best to help them determine for themselves what they want and honor those inclinations. The funeral home does not usually charge extra for visitation, but includes this in the overall cost. Even if only a few people drop by, their visits can be meaningful and calming to the family. (See also the discussion below, pages 34ff.)

---

*For example, in some Orthodox churches, if the deceased is a pastor the casket faces in a different direction.
**See "at the gravesite" (page 95 below).

There are pros and cons to holding a visitation. The pros include:

- People have an opportunity to see that the person is really dead. This reality can help acceptance and moving on.

- The spouse and family have one more chance to experience the warmth of caring community through presence, words of condolence, even deep conversations.

Among the cons:

- The exhausted suffering family has to deal with meeting a lot of people at a time when they may prefer to be alone.

In recent years, it has become more common for visitation hours to take place during the afternoon rather than the evening. The family's decision in this regard should be made in consideration of what hours are likely to be most convenient for those who will attend. If, for example, a very elderly person has died, one who had a number of friends who generally do not drive at night, then the afternoon hours can work well. If, on the other hand, the deceased person had many family members and friends who have to go to work during the day, then the evening is better. Of course sometimes it is possible to hold a visitation that begins in the (daylight) afternoon hours and goes to early evening, after-work hours, say 4:00 to 7:00 p.m.

■ the obituary

An obituary in the local paper is expected and has to be written and sent in rather quickly following the death. Most newspaper obituaries do not come cheap. Charges are typically by the word or line and the price can add up quickly. Still, the obituary is a tribute and also a document that is often kept and treasured over the years by family. In many cities, the newspapers will put in a very short obituary without cost — one that lists only certain details such as name, dates of birth and death, family names, organizations of which the deceased was a member, and the date, time, and place of the funeral or memorial service. In most cases, this free short obituary is not sufficient to write about the person's life or to reflect the family's thoughts, and a family opts to place a longer "paid for" obituary in the next few days.

It can prove to be quite a burden for loved ones to produce an accurate and well written obituary on short notice. Yet for some family members, writing it might bring some consolation, as they put together the details of the accomplishments and experiences of their dear one. But it is always good if the deceased has left them accurate information.

It is not a bad idea for you, as a pastor, to invite church members to write up a few facts about themselves that you and also a family member could keep in a file for their obituary. Of course, many people are so actively involved in the business of living (or so much in denial of the inevitable death we all have ahead of us) that they have little or no interest in making any advance funeral preparations. That is fine. Others feel that they have come to a time in their lives when they are interested and willing to make such preparations, particularly when they realize how helpful this can be to their families.

If you are asked to help with writing an obituary, keep in mind the style and personality of the deceased, and stay within that tradition. Some family members are over-emotional in the written words they choose to describe their loved one, and some tend to exaggerate the person's accomplishments. Other times, an obituary will seem too cold and academic. There are many ways to say the same thing. Asking the family what the deceased might have preferred can keep the tone appropriate. Finally, if you have a hand in writing the obituary, if possible do not leave out the names of any estranged members of the immediate family.

■ purchasing a cemetery plot

Individual plots

Individual plots can be purchased years in advance or right up to the time they are needed. Just like any other plot of land, the cost will vary according to the value at that location. You might suggest that the family check out the location of any plot they plan to purchase. Not every plot is in a scenic spot shaded by a perfect weeping willow tree. Some may be crowded together with other plots, or in an odd location. These plots, of course, are as good as any, as long as the family is comfortable with them.

Family plots

When someone purchases a larger piece of land in a cemetery, commonly known as a family plot, it is likely that person has in mind exactly which family members are to be buried there. The large plot is often for themselves, a spouse, parents, aunts and uncles, children, and sometimes even people who have lived with or who have been in the service of the family for many years. Those who actually end up buried in the family plot are not always these same people. For many reasons, burials do not always go as planned. For example, although in the past people lived in one part of the country most of their lives, today they are constantly moving. Also, people used to stay married to the same person for a lifetime, whereas today many divorce and remarry. Whoever is in possession of the rights to the family plot at any given time will be the decision maker with regard to whose remains go into that plot. Because of the above reasons, and because cremation is becoming more common, spaces in family plots are not always used these days. It is also often the case that a person who has a second spouse, after the death of a first, will still want to be buried alongside the original spouse. In my experience the second spouse nearly always understands and accepts that decision — sometimes because there is a family plot, sometimes because of the children, and sometimes because the first marriage was a very long and happy one.

Burying one body on top of another

Today it can be possible to have one body buried (approximately) twelve feet under, leaving space for a second body to be placed above the first in that same plot. This saves the cost of a second plot, and of a second headstone, although there are extra fees. The headstone will be engraved with the name of the first to die and the second name is added when the second person dies. Sometimes the second name and birth date are added at the time of the first death and only the death date is left to be added when needed.

Cost of digging frozen ground in winter

When death occurs in the winter in a northern climate, there may be extra fees for having to dig the grave with special machines that go through frozen ground (e.g., in Winnipeg, Canada). In other places, it may be more common for the body to be held at the funeral home until the ground thaws (e.g., Connecticut or Maine) and have a spring interment.

■ when a body is to be transported

Many people who die are already owners of a cemetery plot. If this plot is in another location, the body has to be shipped. Be sure the family understands what they are getting into financially. In these cases, they will be required to pay the cost of funeral homes at both ends, as well as the cost of shipping and delivery of the body. It may be more practical simply to purchase a local plot and either sell the first one or let it remain empty. Such situations often lead to emotional discussions, and families often choose to ship the body even though it is quite expensive to do so — the desire to meet requests expressed earlier by the deceased often overriding the expense of transporting the body. The family is not likely to be offended if you, as pastor, at least bring up the subject of potential transport costs. They may also be very grateful if you have helped them to save money they may need in the future.

■ dividing the ashes

Family members often request that portions of the ashes be scattered or placed in different locations. There is no reason why this cannot be done, as long as it is agreed upon by the appropriate family members and, if necessary, the landowners. The reasons for this request vary. A second spouse may have a desired place for the ashes while the children want the ashes placed in or on a family plot. Sometimes the deceased has requested that half the ashes be placed with the first spouse and the other half with the second spouse. Sometimes the deceased has spent retirement in a southern state but still wants also to "rest" in the northern home state. It is best if this decision can be made before the ashes are delivered. Otherwise, you as pastor may end up having to place or scatter half of the ashes and then give the other half to the family to deliver to another location.

■ prearranged funerals

Many will tell us that it is a good idea to arrange and pay for one's own funeral well in advance. This may be true. There are a few precautions to be taken, of course, as with any major purchase. So if you are asked for advice in this regard from one of your church members, there are a few points you can make. First, there is the matter of inflation. This can be a positive side to prearranging a funeral. The specific value of items and services that are paid for in advance could rise substantially by the time the person passes away. In this respect it can be a good value. On the other hand, the money given to the funeral home could have been invested, so one cannot really know in advance which is better financially. More important, perhaps, is the opportunity for the purchaser to make decisions that, otherwise, would be made after that person's death by someone else. Another possible problem with purchasing a prearranged funeral is that the services may not be available at the time you die. We really don't know how long we will live, no matter what the circumstances. So it is important to be sure the funeral home that is chosen expects to be in business and able to provide the service when the time comes or that the agreement will "roll over" to a sister funeral home. It will also be important for the person who purchases the prearranged services to leave detailed information with the family to be sure all the services paid for are actually later provided. Making sure the family has such advance information also prevents the mistake of engaging another funeral home unawares. If a person is going to purchase prearranged services, there will also be the opportunity to "shop around," compare prices, and make a wise and informed choice.

One possibly negative aspect of a prearranged funeral is that the family does not have the opportunity to participate in the decision making. Loved ones often find solace in the simple acts of choosing a hymn or passage of scripture or deciding on a casket. They may even be consoled by making their financial contributions to the cost of a service.

3

 ## the family at the service

■ the spouse at the funeral

THEOLOGICAL REFLECTION

Then the man said "This at last is bone of my bones and flesh of my flesh.... Therefore a man leaves his father and his mother and clings to his wife and they become one flesh." And the man and his wife were both naked and they were not ashamed. (Gen. 2:23a, 24–25)

Many see the marital relationship as the closest that any worldly human relationship can come to the covenant relationship between ourselves and God. As this text from Genesis so poetically proclaims, it is as deep as one's own bones and flesh. There is no other person who can really fathom the profound mutual understanding that can exist between two people in a marital relationship, especially one that has lasted for many decades through thick and thin. Even they themselves will be hard put to try to explain it. It is as if they really have become one. Together they have found a way to be in the world. They protect each other. Each one of the two performs particular tasks for the two of them and, together, they present themselves to the rest of the world as a team, as a family. When a partner in this kind of relationship dies, the beloved spouse will feel an emptiness that is like no other experience. It is described by those who are willing to talk about it as if there is a big hole inside the pit of the stomach and, of course, a pain that they believe will never subside. The final verse of Githa Sowerby's poem "Love Me" describes in simple terms how, after the death, the love continues but in a different way:

Love me for the empty room that I leave behind me.
Love me for the face that's gone and the tears that blind thee.
Love me for the years we knew, the sadness and the laughter.
Love me with the broken heart, and the silence after.

No pastor or any person can really know or understand what the spouse is feeling at the funeral or memorial service. It is truly amazing how most spouses are able to sit through the service of their loved one with such dignity and grace. Sometimes they are in so much grief that they are numbed. Sometimes they are distracted by the busyness of preparations for the service and will feel most of their grief later, after the friends have left. Spouses will often express later that they were able to get through the service only because they were so moved by the outpouring of love and caring from the friends and family who attended. They say they were moved by the service in honor of their loved one and that the pastor's sincere words meant more to them than they can express.

With today's configurations of families, situations arise in which the spouse is not the parent of the children and, in some cases, may not even know the children well. The deceased, for example, may have remarried after the passing of the first spouse or divorce and have, in later years, resided with the new spouse in some distant region. For this reason, some funerals are arranged by the children, and the spouse is by no means the center of attention. In these cases, you as pastor can help meet the needs of the spouse and help the spouse to feel welcome and cared for.

parents at the funeral

THEOLOGICAL REFLECTION _____

The king [David] was deeply moved and went up to the chamber over the gate, and wept; and as he went, he said "O my son Absalom, my son, my son Absalom! Would I have died instead of you, O Absalom, my son, my son!"

(2 Sam. 18:33)

When a child is lost, there is no consolation for the parent. It is profound that the Bible shares with us how King David, with all his power and his connection with God, still suffered just like any other bereaved parent. And David, like so many parents, wished only that it was he who had died instead.

When someone dies, we always hope that the person has lived a long and full life. Frankly, death is easier to tolerate if this is the case. Parents, by nature, are expected to die before their children. There is little that can be more painful than to have to live through the death of one's own child, and yet, of course, it happens. Even when the child is already an adult or even an older adult, living parents will suffer beyond measure. This will be the case with birth parents, adoptive parents, and step-parents.

Step-parents who are the spouses of a birth or adoptive parent of the deceased may not have even raised the child who has died, but they will at the very least be primary care givers for their spouse, the grieving parent, during this sad time. As the pastor, you may or may not know these parents. Try to get to know them a bit if you do not already, as it will help you to choose the right words for the service and also in any later counseling you offer to try to bring them comfort and hope.

siblings of the deceased (and step-siblings) at the funeral

Most siblings will be sincerely grieving, but not all. Depending on the reason for death and whether the death was expected, siblings may be in shock or may be quite prepared for the death. Their behavior will be affected by these differences.

You will also have to deal with the matter of how the siblings relate to each other. They may be taking various roles in the funeral service. They may be assigned by you or other family members to watch over the bereaved parent, a family member who is suffering deep grief, someone with health related problems, or a child. The siblings, in most cases, will already have figured out by the time they see you just who can best handle these kinds of jobs, and they will let you know. Remember, the siblings know each other well, with a lifetime of experience together. Follow their lead. There may be some siblings who are so deeply saddened that they can attend but do not feel able to take any kind of leadership role in the service.

Each sibling typically has quite a different experience of the same parent. The eldest sibling is often the one who chooses to take on responsibility. The middle child is often the comedian of the family, and the youngest is often the one who has been protected or over-protected by the others.

The sibling relationships can be most interesting when one sibling has stayed home to care for the ageing parent or parents over the years while the others have moved forward with their lives, careers, and travels. In my experience, there is sometimes contention, spoken or unspoken, between the sibling who stayed home and those who moved away. Let me explain. The sibling who has stayed home may harbor some resentment toward the one or more who have moved away. Such a person may express to you, the pastor, a sure feeling of having understood what the parent wanted and a pride in always having been there to help and provide when the other siblings were nowhere to be found. Siblings who return at the time of the death of the parent, or after the death, have been known to carry a fair amount of guilt about their lack of participation in caring for the elderly parent. They may attempt to make up for their absence by offering all kinds of advice on how the "home body" sibling should have handled the parent's affairs, as well as how the funeral should be arranged. This advice is not always gratefully received. You may well hear variations on, "I spent all these years caring for mother. Where was my sibling then?" from the stay-at-home sibling. You might respond by simply pointing out what good care the home sibling has taken of the parent and then also suggest that the sibling who has returned for the funeral may be feeling badly and, for this reason, trying to make up for it at an inopportune time. The home sibling will nearly always appreciate any praise you offer and will try to understand the situation of the returning siblings.

■ grandparents, great grandparents, and step-grandparents

A death is nearly always very hard for grandparents and great grandparents. To begin with, older people expect to die first. It is unnatural for a person to lose a grandchild or great grandchild. We like to think that, when we are ready to die, our progeny will survive, in some way living for us and for all we have stood for in life. Such elderly people are often grieving doubly, deeply sad for the sake of their children who are now the parents of a deceased child.

■ some age-related matters

SCENARIO _____

Madelyn was not that surprised when she heard that her brother Dan had died. After all, he was ninety-four. She was only eighty-seven and in pretty good health, so she made arrangements to fly to the funeral. She stayed with her older sister, Marge, who was ninety. Even though there was the sadness of saying goodbye to their beloved brother Dan, Madelyn and Marge took some pleasure in being together and in the company of their still living brother, Henry. Henry too had lived a long life. He was ninety-two and in pretty good shape. There was little doubt that they were one long-lived family. The day following the service, they were all together in Marge's kitchen having a bite of lunch and chatting together about their shared childhoods. Brother Henry slipped out for a cigarette. When he was about to come back in, he walked up the three cement steps, grabbed for the screen door, missed, fell backwards onto the cement, hit his head, and died instantly. So it turned out that Madelyn stayed with Marge for another week and they buried one more brother. As the Bible says, "Keep awake therefore, for you do not know on what day your Lord is coming" (Matt. 24:42).

With the elderly members of the deceased's family, there may be health-related issues to consider in advance of the funeral. You, the family, and the funeral home people if necessary can sit down together and consider ways to make the elderly more comfortable. There may be older family members who will do better at the service if they have a younger person from the family assigned to attend them, just to keep an eye out for any special needs. These persons may also want to go to the cemetery or memorial garden and then back to the reception. You might arrange for chairs to be set outside for them in advance. Sometimes an elderly or infirm family member will just stay at the church or go directly to the place of the reception instead of also attending the gathering at the cemetery. People know their limits.

If there will be a lot of older people at the service, be sure that everyone who is speaking is correctly instructed in using the sound system.

■ those who have traveled distances

Often a service will have to be pushed out a day or two so that particular people can travel from long distances. When they arrive, they will need a place to stay. Will they stay with the spouse of the deceased, the siblings, or other close family members? Depending on the family dynamics, their presence at this difficult time could be either a help or an added burden. If the spouse or family members are asking for your advice, try to get them to determine what they really want and then encourage them to be honest with the visiting family about whether they should go to a hotel. It is likely the visiting people will understand.

■ ex-spouses at the funeral

It is generally difficult for ex-spouses to decide whether to attend the funeral or memorial service. Their decision will depend on many factors, including the following: How many years were they married to this person? Was the marriage generally a good one that ended because they changed as circumstances changed? Are there shared children between the deceased and the ex-spouse? Would those children want and expect the ex-spouse to be present? If these children (young or adults) will be suffering a lot with their grief, would they find the presence of the living parent to be a consolation at the service or a distraction? And, most important, how might any current spouse of the deceased react to the presence of this ex-spouse at the service?

When there is a current spouse, should the ex-spouse call and ask for permission to attend? Each ex-spouse will have to decide whether this is appropriate. There is, of course, no law specifying who can attend. In some ways a funeral is a public event. Most obituary notices list the place and time of the service, so the invitation is open. Still, the presence of an ex-spouse could cause pain to the current spouse, who is already likely to be suffering greatly. On the other hand, the ex-spouse may truly want to say goodbye and to remember and honor any happy years the two had shared. This, perhaps, can be done just as well at home, without attending the service. In many ways the goodbyes have already taken place at the time of the divorce.

The ex-spouse may be concerned for his or her children and want to be with them in their grief at the loss of their other parent. You, as pastor, might suggest as an option that the ex-spouse can visit with the children at some other appointed time, when they will meet to share memories of the deceased and remember happier times they spent together.

At any rate, if the ex-spouse does attend the funeral, it is usually a good idea that this person keeps a low profile and does not linger, unless the current and the ex-spouse have established a positive relationship. As the pastor, you will not control any of these things, but it is good to be aware of them so you can treat all parties with the care and respect they need.

■ relatives who are estranged

THEOLOGICAL REFLECTION _____

Abraham breathed his last and died in a good old age, an old man and full of years, and was gathered to his people. His sons Isaac and Ishmael buried him...with his wife Sarah. (Gen. 25:8–10)

At first, this passage may seem perfectly usual. An old man is buried by his two sons. But those who are familiar with the earlier part of this family's story will recognize the deep pathos. We are presented with a picture of two estranged brothers, one the son of Abraham's wife, Sarah, and the other the son of her Egyptian maid, Hagar. Here, now, at the death of their father, the two sons are again together, to share the task of burying their father. Whatever the feelings each may have toward this father they share, whatever relationship now exists between the two sons, they have a job to do together. Their work in getting their father properly laid to rest will surely call up profound memories for both. This time that by tradition they are now required to share may put them farther apart or bring them closer. When the work of burying their father begins, nobody knows how it will be for the half brothers. In the story, the outcome is left to the reader's imagination. The text only tells us that God blessed Isaac (Gen. 25:11) and then that Ishmael too had many descendants (Gen. 25:12).

You are unlikely to know why family estrangements have taken place. Sometimes there has been a serious breech while other times the reasons may even have been forgotten. The family may determine that a low profile is a good idea for a particular relative. Yet the disenfranchised themselves may not feel this way. Should any estranged relatives show up at the service, it is good for you to take a bit of time to chat with them. The rest of the family may not be thrilled, but it is very likely the estranged person went through a considerable struggle about whether to come and may be feeling quite uncomfortable. Your words can only help.

■ people who are like family

Many people have friends who are much closer to them than their own families. Sometimes a dear friend not related to a person in any way may have shared a lifetime with the deceased and may really love that person. In some cases, this friend has cared for the deceased over many years of illness, or has been like a mother or a sibling, like a daughter or son, or even a spouse. (In many states, but not all, "common-law" marriage is recognized by law.) These people need special attention from you because they will be in grief. It is especially difficult for some of them when, at the time of the funeral, they are cast aside or ignored by the legitimate family members. (This happens more often than people realize.) Officially and legally, it is always the closest family members who make the decisions with regard to the matters of the deceased (unless the person who died has made specific legal arrangements that say otherwise). You as pastor may find yourself torn at times between ministering to deeply caring friends of the deceased and, sometimes, dealing with less than caring family members. Usually family members will readily accept the "friend," but that is not always the case. In the end, you will have to be very clear about the need for you to follow the wishes of the persons appointed to make the decisions about the funeral, while also being sensitive to the needs of those suffering the most when these parties are not one and the same.

SCENARIO _____

> Pastor Jim didn't know what he was getting into when he agreed to perform a funeral service for Madge. The first person whose name he was given by the funeral home was of Madge's next door neighbor, Jennifer. Madge's son, he was told, was on his

way and would arrive from out of town one hour before the service. So in order to get things started, Pastor Jim called Jennifer the good neighbor and said, "Tell me about your friend Madge." Madge, said Jennifer, had been a thoughtful, caring, and loving person who enjoyed her friends and took particular delight in her garden. Pastor Jim was impressed and wrote a fine funeral sermon about this caring and dear deceased woman.

The next day, just before the funeral, her son arrived. Pastor Jim was surprised to find him gruff and angry. "Look, reverend or whatever you call yourself! I'm not into religion and all this emotional stuff. To be honest, my mother didn't please me much. I'm here to get her buried and meet with the lawyer. So just say as little as possible and let's get on with it. The sooner it's over, the better." Pastor Jim was taken aback. This was not the loving son he'd been expecting. Was Madge the person her neighbor said she was? Certainly, Pastor Jim didn't and couldn't know. So after some thought he said to the son, "We really don't have to have this funeral if you don't want to. I was asked by the funeral director, and I am doing my job." The son replied, "Oh, you might as well go ahead." So after holding back his negative feelings and pulling himself together, Pastor Jim decided to put on the funeral that would be most helpful to Jennifer, the neighbor, and any other friends who had come to say their farewells. As for the son, well, maybe he needed to hear some good things about his mother, whether he wanted to or not. Truth be told, Pastor Jim even dragged it out a bit. He talked at length about the beautiful gardens Madge had lovingly tended, about her friends who cared for her, and about what a loss her death would be to all who loved her. After the service, the son predictably left without a word. Had Pastor Jim done the right thing? He didn't know. Sometimes only God knows.

4

 caring for the immediate
family

■ pastor's "who's who": remembering names, roles, and relationships

Even the most seasoned pastor can find it difficult to keep track of all the new names that come up when preparing for a funeral. In most cases you will know the exact full name of the deceased along with at least one or two family members. The most important name is of course that of the deceased. If he or she is someone you knew personally, you probably will have the name right. If not, be sure to ask the spouse and family members by which name this person was known. Otherwise you might find yourself repeating the name Edward when the person had been known all his life as Eddy. Worse yet, you may be burying Sylvester when everyone in his life knew him as Biff. Also, many people go through their lives using their middle name, or sometimes only initials. (Remember J.R.?) Be sure to ask! An additional problem arises when the spouse has called the person by one name and other family members call them by another. You can deal with this easily by clarifying the two names and then, from that point, settling with the family on which to use.

You will also likely be speaking the names of the family members. Nearly always, there are many whose names you are hearing for the first time when you meet with the family to prepare the service. It is perfectly acceptable to ask for and then write down their names (and how to pronounce them) and their relationship to the deceased. You should also always check out the obituary to be sure you have all the names and relationships correct. Some obituaries will list only the names of the deceased's children and grandchildren but not their partners. It is best if you use the word "spouse" when asking about them, as there is always the possibility that some may be in gay or lesbian relationships. That way, nobody will be offended and they will be more comfortable in telling you.

■ helping the family before the day of the service

Funeral services are traditionally two or three days after the death, but with memorial services on the upswing because cremation is increasing it can be several weeks and sometimes even months before the service takes place. In such circumstances, after your initial contact or personal visit with the family, it is good to keep in touch during any interim period as best you can without intruding on their grieving.

Sometimes family members, especially a spouse, will express to you that they do not know how they will get through the service without breaking down. It can help simply to say that, in your experience, somehow, people always get through it. They will be given the strength they need. Just hearing this seems to help them manage when the time comes.

5

 the wake, viewing, or visitation time

The title of this prefuneral event varies from country to country, state to state, and also sometimes among religious or ethnic traditions. For example, "wake" is the word usually used for a Roman Catholic visitation time in which the body is viewed, the family are greeted and consoled, and prayers are led by the priest.

A Protestant visitation time is similar but does not often include an organized prayer time. Still, the pastor usually is present, at least if the deceased has been a member of the church.

■ advice for the family

It is generally a good idea for the family to hold some sort or viewing, wake, or visitation. If the body has been embalmed, it will often be shown, but not always. At this event, people have the opportunity to say their goodbyes, talk to each other, and prepare themselves emotionally for the service that will usually take place the next day.

Such an event, in which the body is displayed in a casket, may be welcomed by family and friends or may be incredibly difficult for them. The attitudes toward this tradition of embalming, visitation with the body displayed, and burial vary from area to area. It is my experience as a pastor that, in south Florida, where cremation seems more often to be the norm, friends sometimes seemed really uncomfortable attending an actual viewing and being expected to come forward and gaze at the body of the deceased. In certain of the more northern climes, on the other hand, I have seen people surprised and confused if they did not see the body displayed.

In the case of the Roman Catholic community, prayers will be led by the local priest. If you are a Protestant pastor, there is no reason why you too might not lead the gathered group in prayer. If they are willing and able, let the family take the lead in making the decisions about any prayer time. Often, even a short prayer from you can be of great comfort. Yet there are some visitations where a prayer with the entire group just won't work. People are often chatting in different groups or even different rooms, or are lined up in a long hallway waiting to speak with the family. There may just be too many people for you to get their attention. So do not feel prayer is an absolute necessity. Your denominational and community traditions can also offer guidance. You might choose to offer a prayer with the immediate family, either before the people arrive or after they have gone.

■ will you attend?

If the deceased is a member of your church, you will probably be expected to attend the visitation. It is not necessary in most cases for you to stay for the entire time. Everyone knows pastors have busy schedules, and often you will have to be getting away to finish writing your funeral sermon. It is probably best if you arrive early, shortly before the others. This way you can accompany the family into the room when they first view the body if they would like you to be there. Seeing the body of a loved one lying in a casket can be traumatic. It could well be the most important time you spend with the spouse and family. Often the body has been prepared by funeral directors who have never met the person, and the deceased may not look the way the family expects.

■ how to be useful if you go

While at the visitation, you will have the opportunity to talk with members of the extended family as well as friends of the deceased. If the family has needs during the visitation, you may be able to communicate with the funeral directors on their behalf.

At most visitations for church members, some fellow church members are sure to be attending. Your presence affords you the opportunity to minister to them in a variety of ways, as well as to the family, which, of course, will be your main focus.

6

 **family's involvement
in the service**

■ family participation in the service —
the benefits and the challenges

There are many ways family members can participate in the funeral or memorial service. In years past, family members in funeral chapels were often secluded in a separate side room, or behind a curtain. This way their grieving would not be witnessed by others who attended the service. In our modern times, family is usually seated in the front pews and some even take an active part in the service. Some will find that participation greatly helps them in their grieving. Others may need to simply sit and experience the worship, receiving the words of consolation. The family members will let you know their preferences.

■ a display of photos of the deceased

Family members often put together a collage of special photos of the deceased. The photos can be displayed on a table, in binders, or on some kind of bulletin board in the funeral home, narthex, or church hall where the reception takes place. Those who attend the service seem to really appreciate a photo display. Photos provide the opportunity for guests to view pictures of the deceased and family in happier days and in various stages of the life journey, and thus prompt conversation among people who may otherwise find it difficult to begin to talk.

■ funeral bulletins that include the participation of family

For most funerals held in a church, there will be a bulletin or program that includes the order of service. It is becoming more common for family to be involved, providing content and sometimes even in printing up the programs themselves. The bulletins may include a poem, favorite scripture passage, some special logo or photo on the front cover, or a picture and biography of the deceased on the back page.

■ inviting others to speak

Spouses and other family members have usually decided before they meet with you whether or not they wish to speak at the service, or have another family member speak.

The number of people who speak varies among cultures and even, at times, from state to state. In certain areas of the South, for example, there are churches where it is common and expected for anyone in the congregation to be invited to say a few words about the deceased toward the end of the service. One reason for this is that, in churches that consist mainly of retired "snowbirds" from the North, the church community, in some profound ways, takes the place of family. For this reason it becomes the norm for fellow church members and friends to want to say a few words. In certain parts of the Northeast, on the other hand, perhaps because of traditions of stoicism, it is nearly always requested by families that only the pastor speak.

Reading scripture

A family member or close friend may be invited by the family to read from scripture. The scripture reader or readers should receive the passage in advance of the service so they have the opportunity to read it over and prepare. Some will need enlarged copies.

Giving a eulogy

The eulogy is the most logical place for a chosen family member or friend to speak. The family should be offered this option. Usually, their reaction to this question will be strong and immediate. On most occasions, the family will agree on who will speak. One potential problem is that you and this eulogist could end up saying some of the same things about the deceased. This is not a big problem. Unless you both go into identical details, it is not inappropriate for people to hear remembrances and stories from two different angles. Still, it doesn't hurt, should you have the chance, to discuss with this person some of what you will be saying, so that you can steer clear of the things the other person plans to say. Of course, you don't want to put eulogists on the spot, in case they have not yet decided what they will be saying at the funeral.

The loved one who offers to give the eulogy will usually be someone who can handle this job. Still, no matter how experienced at public speaking this person may be, it would be good for you to offer a polite but fairly strong reminder to keep the eulogy relatively short. The best way to explain this to the person is to offer a few facts such as the following: (1) a twenty-minute talk is only five pages double spaced, so if you plan to speak for ten minutes, a couple of pages should do it. (2) If you are giving your eulogy extemporaneously, then be especially careful. When you begin to reflect on the past, time tends to stand still; you might think you were speaking for eight minutes when, in fact, it was twenty minutes or more.

SCENARIO _____

> Their father had died and the two brothers and Mom were left. The family decided that it was definitely Brother George who would say a few words in remembrance of his beloved father. The pastor coached George, with her carefully worded advice that he should keep the eulogy relatively short, as the planned service was already quite lengthy. She explained to him that, in her experience, these remembrances often took much longer than the person

speaking realized. The time came for George to speak. He nervously rose to the podium. In his hands were a rather large number of file cards. On each card he had written only a sentence or a few words. The pastor started to relax. She figured it might be ten minutes max, and sat back in her seat to listen. Ten minutes passed as George spoke, then ten minutes more, and ten minutes more. How would the pastor end what was becoming a lengthy dissertation on the virtues of George's father? What had happened was this. Each short sentence of each little index card represented one memory George had of his father. The problem was that, once he began to reflect on the good times he'd shared with his dear dad, he lost all track of time. To put it theologically, George had entered into kairos time. This was great for George, and possibly even for his family. But for the rest, it was much more information than they needed. They had planned the service to be up to an hour in length; now it was clearly going well beyond that. Finally, the pastor decided she had to step in, but how would she do this without offending? She stood up, smiling, and moved toward George. Finally, he seemed to snap out of his reverie and looked up at her. He wound down at last and the pastor slipped in and thanked him for his fine words. The service, blessedly, came to an end.

■ performing music

It is usually difficult for a family member or close friend to perform music at a funeral, but it can be done. Music touches the heart deeply, not only for the listener but for the performer. If a speaker who is reading a text breaks down and cannot go on, then someone else can take over and read the material. But if a musician stops in the middle of performing the music, it is not likely that anyone can take over. Will the person be able to complete the performance of the music prepared for the service? They will know best. If they are able to focus on the task at hand and on the good the music is doing for others, they should be all right. If, when the time comes, they do stop in mid-song, people will surely understand and you can simply wait or go ahead with the rest of the service as seems appropriate.

■ remembering other loved ones who have died, or those who cannot attend

At a funeral it is natural that people will be remembering others they have loved who have also passed away. It may be appropriate to say a few words about those others who have died. If the deceased is widowed, the spouse who predeceased should definitely be spoken about. If the deceased had lost a child, then it will likely be appropriate that the child's name be spoken as well. It is always fitting to recall "all those who have gone before us, who we remember now."

part two

on the day
of the service

7

 ## setting the scene:
before the service

■ preparing the sanctuary

Your church likely has a custodian or other staff member whose
responsibility it is to make sure the place is tidy and clean. Funerals are not part of the regular weekly schedule and might be
taking place almost any time or day of the week. Be sure to let
your custodian know in advance. This way the person can be
sure all bulletins from your last service have been picked up, the
floors cleaned, and so forth. In most churches, the custodian will
be given a list every week of what events are coming but, in some
smaller churches, it may be the pastor who takes care of these

things. Just as in your home, where you'd like things especially tidy when guests are coming, you will want the church to look good. An attractive church is simply good hospitality.

There may be special altar cloths to be laid out or candles to be lit for the service. Generally, any altar cloths and banners that are being used for the liturgical season will be appropriate for the funeral. If the banners are particularly joyful or light-hearted, they may not be right for a time of mourning. You can decide along with your deacons, altar guild, or other church leaders if these need to be changed or any furniture removed. If a casket is to be brought in, sometimes some sanctuary furnishings do need to be moved. Be sure the racks in the narthex that hold any brochures and newsletters about your church are neat and well lit. People often stop by and find these to be of interest.

■ the guestbook

If a funeral home is at all involved, it is very likely that the funeral director will provide a guestbook. It is good if you have a lectern or stand on which the book can be placed in the narthex or entranceway to the sanctuary. This way, the book can be placed in a strategic location, along with a good pen so that people may sign, either on their way in or out of the service. These books are much appreciated by the bereaved, especially when they look them over much later and see who was in attendance. On the day of the service, they are often in far too much pain to really take note of all the people present.

■ the flowers

Funerals nowadays are not usually as overwhelmed with dozens upon dozens of flower arrangements as they were in years past. Often, families will request, toward the end of the obituary notice, that in lieu of flowers donations be made to organizations or charities with which the deceased had a particular connection, in their living or in their dying. Sometimes there are no flowers at all at a funeral, and this is perfectly acceptable. The florists generally call the church office to ask when arrangements can be delivered, so you or your secretary or a volunteer will arrange to have a church door open for their arrival. If a church has a lot of weddings and funerals, arrangements are sometimes made with local florists to provide them a key, so they can come and go with such deliveries even when no church official or secretary is present.

An hour or so before the service, you may want to go into the sanctuary or chapel where the service will take place just to check things over. See that the flowers have been set in appropriate places. You will know what locations offer the best use of the space.

When the service is over (and the reception, if it is at the church), you might want to remind family members about the flowers and ask if they plan to take them home. It is usually best to ask someone other than the spouse or closest loved one, as this person will have enough on his or her mind. You will know by this stage whom to ask. Some families opt to take the flowers to their homes or the gravesite; others prefer that you use them to decorate the church on Sunday or that you take them to someone homebound or in the hospital. This is often not the best choice: flowers for the upcoming Sunday service have usually already been donated and dedications already printed in the Sunday bulletin, in honor or memory of someone else. You might also find it physically uncomfortable to personally cart a large floral arrangement out of the church, into your car, and then into someone's hospital room. Besides, they often have a "funeral arrangement" look about them. Still, the gesture to give the flowers has been a kind one on the part of the family. If they really want to leave them at the church, graciously accept. The flowers might be used to beautify the church fellowship hall or other space. Sometimes they can be disassembled and smaller bouquets made up to be delivered to the sick.

■ gathering the family for prayer

Do not worry about anything, but in everything by prayer and supplication with thanksgiving let your requests be made known to God. And the peace of God which passes all understanding will guard your hearts and your minds in Christ Jesus. (Phil. 4:6–7)

Whether or not the family of the bereaved is a "praying" family, they are sure to appreciate your words of prayer; at your meetings with them and then also at the service. As this passage from Philippians so beautifully puts it, whatever deep worries we may have, God knows and understands. God promises us peace, a kind of peace that surpasses all human understanding, and that will come in God's time.

When you speak to the immediate family on the day or evening before the service, suggest they arrive in your office no later than twenty minutes prior to the service. Be sure to tell the ushers or any who may be watching at the door to direct the immediate family members to your office. When they have arrived, you can welcome them personally. Once they are gathered, offer a short prayer, check to see if they have any concerns, and then lead them into the sanctuary a few minutes before the service is to begin. This short gathering will give the family a few minutes to be together before they have to face everyone. If any are really nervous, weeping, or upset, your gathering prayer can offer consolation. A prayer that focuses on God's presence through times of trial, or on the comfort that worship is sure to bring in times of sorrow, can be powerful and helpful.

8

 **the family enters
the sanctuary**

Find out in advance of the service approximately how many
people constitute the immediate family members who will be
seated together in the sanctuary. Be sure the required seating
area has been cordoned off with a wide ribbon or with "re-
served" signs on the pews or seats. Many funerals have much
larger turnouts than expected, and you have to be sure there are
plenty of seats for the family, as they will be entering last.

The time arrives when the service is about to begin. If you are
in a funeral chapel, the family will likely all have been seated in
advance by the funeral directors. If the service is in your church,
it will usually be you who leads them to their seats. You will
walk with the immediate family members through the church
from your office to the narthex and into the sanctuary. Once
they are seated comfortably, you can then proceed to your position at the lectern or pulpit or before the altar or communion
table. The spouse, if there is one, will be seated at the end of
the front pew nearest you (or in the second pew if the first is
to stay empty). Seated beside the spouse in most circumstances
will be a daughter, son, or sibling (or even a friend if this is the
spouse's closest person). The family members will usually just
naturally seat themselves in the order that is the most comfortable for them. You might watch, however, for any relatives who
arrive late or need special seating. In the case of a service in remembrance of a child who has died, there are likely also to be
grandparents in the family group. At some funerals, the close
family can be pretty large.

9

 the importance of
the pastor's words

Because of the suffering of the bereaved, it is possible that they may not really hear or remember the actual words you speak in memory of their loved one. Most likely, it will be your demeanor, your kindness, and the understanding you show to them at this time of confusion and pain that will stay in their hearts and minds. Still, your words are also important — your words in the sermon or eulogy, and also your words before and after the service to the family and those they love. In some respects you even become like a parent figure. You're the one they depend on to see that the service goes well and that it is befitting their loved one. You are also their prime comforter in assuring them that, in this time of chaos, God at least has everything in order.

SCENARIO

It had taken many years before Brian had admitted, even to himself, that he was going to spend his life and career as a classical singer. He was perfectly aware of the cold fact that such a life would very likely not bring him fame, fortune, or probably even a decent living. Still, singing was too big a part of him to be set aside for just a day job or made into some weekend hobby. So the struggle had begun. He entered a music conservatory on scholarship but was still finding himself without money to meet many of his needs. He had been told by his voice teacher that, however many lessons he took, it would only be performing in public as a singer that would really help him grow in his art and, over time, become a professional.

With this in mind, Brian had accepted a position as soloist in a church that was not of his own denomination. Just at the time that he was hesitatingly getting started, tragedy hit his life. Brian's beloved father died. At the conclusion of his father's funeral, he (being the only son) approached his pastor and thanked him for the fine funeral service. His pastor's response was this. "Young man, I hear that you're singing in churches that are not of our denomination! This is not the way you were raised. You should know better." The pastor then turned on his heels and walked away. The pastor very likely felt justified, thinking he had done his job in attempting to bring this young man of his flock back into line. The pain of this insensitive moment on the part of the pastor lasted a lifetime for the young singer. Brian could not and did not give up his life's goal to be a singer, and he did not quit his church job. But his faith and trust in his own home church had been shattered by his pastor's thoughtless and insensitive words on the day of his father's funeral.

Brian did finally find a home for his faith again, but only after many years and in another place. Brian eventually chose to join a church where people understood and appreciated each other's God-given gifts — and their need to use them.

The funeral is *never* the place to engage in discussions about any matters that could hurt a mourning family member or friend.

■ ways to be sure everyone is welcomed

THEOLOGICAL REFLECTION _____

For my house shall be a place of prayer for all peoples.

(Isa. 56:7)

Churches can start to be more like country clubs with the goal of only serving and pleasing their paying members. When a funeral service is held at your church (or when you are invited to officiate at a service in a funeral home) you will nearly always be leading worship with people from a variety of faith backgrounds. As you speak your chosen words in remembrance of the deceased you will honor both that person and God by showing care and respect for every person who has come to the service.

You can make sure that everyone is made to feel welcome at the service by simply offering words of welcome to them. In the context of these welcoming words, you can remind them too that God loves everyone. Remember, there are likely to be people who are members of other denominations, other faiths, and even people of no faith. Most age groups are likely to be represented. At both weddings and funerals, I often like to say something like this: "Let us remember that, no matter what our age, from the youngest to the oldest here today, we are loved by a God who loves us more than we can ever know."

■ the service is always worship

Be careful not to turn the service into a memorializing (or glorifying) of the deceased. In days gone by families were often disappointed because pastors at the funeral services hardly mentioned their loved one, except perhaps to speak the name once followed by a list of the closest relatives. Since then, many funerals have taken a turn in the opposite direction and become one glorious idealized memory after another of the one now gone. Families will receive much better satisfaction and consolation from a service that offers a balance of praise of the loved one, a time for prayer, music that soothes their suffering, and, most important, scripture reading and words of hope to assure them they can trust in the promises of God. A funeral service is always a worship service.

■ the purpose of a funeral service

Grieving at funerals is threefold: we grieve for the deceased most of all; we grieve also because, at these times, we remember those we love who have died; and finally we grieve at being reminded that we too are mortal.

The grieving

The family's grieving. The spouse, partner, and any immediate family are going to be in a very different state at the service from the others who are gathered. Even though you speak to everyone, your words are primarily addressed to the close family. The rest are generally there to offer support, although some may also be in deep mourning.

Family members should be sure to have handkerchiefs with them, but it is a caring church that places boxes of tissues in the pews. Having said that, generally family members do their heavy weeping at another time and place and try their best to maintain silence and dignity during the service. Occasionally you will run into a family member, or even a spouse or partner, who does not seem to be grieving at all. It is possible that your guess may be right. Nobody but the individual knows the reasons for this and it is, of course, personal business. Not every family member may be grieving: let it go. There is no need to address it in most cases. Some people simply have found no way to express their grief. Others may be angry at the deceased, or even relieved that the death has happened. You may learn the reasons if you are counseling the person at a later time. But the funeral is not the time for digging into matters that are very personal

The friends' grieving. Indeed, we do not always know who is grieving and how much. Some people will attend the funeral simply to pay respects to a friend, a business colleague, or a neighbor. Others may have come as a friend of a family member. So there will inevitably be people at the funeral who are not exactly grieving, but rather are present to lend their support. Others, sometimes those we least expect, may be sincerely devastated. You may be able to tell who these people are by their demeanor, the way they are responding to your words, or their weeping. Just keep in mind that you, as the pastor, never know the whole story of a person's life and relationships. Be sensitive to the presence of suffering, even when it comes from the back pew.

Your own grieving. It is often the case that the deceased is someone you, the pastor, have known, especially if the person was a member of your congregation. You will have had at least some interaction with the deceased and sometimes a lot of time together during the illness that led to death. In addition, if the deceased is a church member, you are very likely to also know and care about the family. If we are honest, we pastors have to admit that we grieve more at some funerals than at others. We can't be bursting into tears when we are the ones in charge of the service. But, if tears do come, there is no need to be embarrassed. Have your tissues ready. If the deceased is someone we cared a lot about, it will be good to take some private time, or time with someone we love and trust, to talk about the person who died, to remember, and then to cry if we need to cry. Taking the time to do this sometime before the service should really help you to stay in control when the time comes for your needed leadership.

The joy of resurrection

THEOLOGICAL REFLECTION _____

And God himself will be with them; he will wipe every tear from their eyes. Death will be no more; mourning and crying and pain will be no more, for the first things have passed away. (Rev. 21:3b–4)

A version of this passage can be found in two places in the Bible, Isaiah 25:8 and Revelation 21:3b–4. In both, the promise is offered in order to give hope to a people who have been saddened by war and years of suffering. The words remind us that weeping and mourning, tears, and pain are, in some sense, always temporary. God's promises to us through Jesus assure us of something better ahead. Another similar passage (Ps. 30:5) says, "Weeping may linger for the night, but joy comes with the morning." Bereaved families may truly not understand so early on in their grief that their suffering will ease with passing time. Still, they will listen to and receive these words of hope from scripture. A day will come, it is promised, when crying shall come to an end.

As pastors, we know how important it is that the sermon leads in some way to the good news of resurrection. In whatever ways are appropriate, you will remind all who have come to the service that, as Christians, we trust that the life of the deceased is not over, but that this person has entered, in some mysterious way, into a new place. We are taught to hope for the promised life with God at the end of this worldly life. It is quite acceptable to say that no person knows any details of what that life after death might be, but that we are people of the promise. You are not expected to speak about things that no person can truly know. Yet, no matter what the level of belief or unbelief of the gathered group, those present look to you for those vital words of hope. They are words that can help build faith in you and those who hear you.

There is little doubt that most people attending a funeral also give some thought while there to their own eventual demise. They are unlikely to talk about it, even with you, unless they have some serious illness and are not expected to live. Still, you can be sure that thoughts about death will be on nearly everyone's mind. They may experience fear, concern about their own religious doubts, or just a sense of curiosity. So to some degree, there is more than one death you are talking about!

Celebrating a life

It is important to most families today that the service not be all weeping and sadness. They want their loved one to be remembered and celebrated in a fitting way. In many cases, certain family members have had past experiences of funerals that were less than glorious, funerals that sent them home feeling worse instead of consoled. They did not hear words of hope and encouragement to trust in the promises of God. So know that, if you make the service a celebration of the life of the deceased, you are already halfway home. It's good if you can use words such as the following on the bulletin cover: "In Memory and Celebration of the Life of Mary Smith." It's good if you can prepare a service that begins with the fact of the death, moving then to reflection on the deceased person's life. Work your way to the theme: the joy of resurrection, the promise of life eternal, and the fact that the deceased is already "home" with God.

There are many ways the service can truly celebrate the life of the deceased, for example, by enumerating the deceased's best qualities, sharing good things the person has said and done.

These could include little acts of caring or ways the person showed his or her love. You can remember the person's excellent work record, or accomplishments in art or crafts, music or poetry. You might want to speak of the person's deep faith or generosity in giving to the church or other organizations. You may choose to talk about how much people liked to be with this person and about how he told great stories or how she baked the best cookies. When you get the right details and speak of things that ring true for those who have come to the service, you will sense a real response from the gathered congregation. You are celebrating the life that the deceased shared with those who have now come to remember, to grieve, and to celebrate. They will appreciate the time you have taken to make the personal connections.

Some families will ask that the service be only a celebration. Some make this request because they are personally uncomfortable with their own grieving and want you to avoid any talk at all about the fact of death. There is no call for you to follow this request in a strict sense. You can keep the service relatively upbeat. But remember, they do need to hear and speak about this death and also to face the fact of death. Underneath their fear, they know there will be talk about death at the service, and they will likely be able to deal with it better than they expect. They are usually not giving themselves enough credit. They are stronger than they trust themselves to be. And besides, dealing with the reality is a crucial part of grieving.

■ choosing scripture readings

The closest loved ones should be given the opportunity to choose at least some of the selections from scripture that will be read at the service. Inquire in a way that will not embarrass the loved ones if they can't think of any scripture passages — for this is often the case. They are distracted by many things at this time. You might simply say that you will pick out some passages and, if they do come up with some others later, just to call and let you know. It is not uncommon to receive a call the next morning.

They may tell you they have looked through their loved one's Bible and found a well-marked passage. Or they may now recall a passage the deceased personally loved or that is special to them and ask that it be included in the service.

Certain passages are beloved at funeral services. Perhaps the most popular Old Testament passage is the Twenty-Third Psalm. Among the most popular New Testament passages are John 14:1–6, "In my Father's house are many rooms..." and Romans 8:14–23, 31–39 "Nothing can separate us from the love of God..." You can, of course, use any verses. If possible, choose scripture readings that are especially relevant to the life and personality of the deceased. Then you can build the sermon around them. The list of scripture readings in the appendix (page 129) offers a few ideas for funerals and can also be presented to family members to prompt their selection.

■ the eulogy/the sermon

If you are the only speaker, you have two options. You can give the eulogy (the words specifically about the life and accomplishments of the deceased) and then, possibly after music, offer a sermon (the words of good news, based on scripture, that our faith teaches). Another option that seems to work better is to weave the two (eulogy and sermon) together. Some positive aspect of the life of the deceased can often present a good example of service or faithfulness. This then can lead you into a short sermon about a life of trust in God and, in turn, the message of God's trustworthiness and faithfulness in the life of this person now deceased. There is generally some part of a person's earthly life that was particularly good. You can bring comfort to the family, speak kindly of their loved one, and also share the good news of scripture.

If someone else is doing the eulogy and you are offering the sermon, it is best not to use this time of suffering to try to coerce people into believing in God or in an afterlife. Yes, they are vulnerable, and many pastors have grabbed at this chance to change hearts. It is, of course, a matter of your own style and your denomination's attitudes. Still, I am convinced that it is the love you offer and the gentle confidence you exude that will bring them closer to God. What they need at this time is not a fiery preacher, but a caring role model of faith.

10

to commune or not to commune

Depending on your church tradition, the family may request communion as part of the service. Holy Communion (the Lord's Supper) is a great source of solace and strength to many Christians. The thing to be considered with serving communion at a funeral or memorial service is that the gathered worshippers will nearly always come from a variety of faith backgrounds. In some instances the church may even have rules that only its members may partake of communion. In other churches, all are invited. Still, people from other churches or non-Christian faith traditions (or no tradition at all) may rightly feel uncomfortable even if they are invited to partake. If the family really wants communion, there are two possibilities. Along with deacons or elders of your church, you might serve it to the immediate family at an earlier time, before the service. Or you could include it as part of the service, offering clear instructions in the funeral bulletin. These would include a sincere invitation along with details about how it is to be served and taken, instructions on where any cups are to be placed after the communion, and some information about the meaning of communion that will help them decide if they wish to partake.

II

 choices regarding music

Pastor Harold was a good guy, but had always been very serious about his theology. When one of his elderly parishioners passed away, he went to the house to talk with the family. The sentimental and grieving daughter made him a cup of tea and they began to put together plans for the service. When Pastor Harold mentioned hymns, the daughter said she knew exactly what her mother had wanted. "We'll have mother's favorite hymn," she pronounced. "It's 'In the Garden.' " Pastor Harold, convinced that he had his theology in order and completely sure that he wanted no bad theology going on in any church he served, took this opportunity to explain to the daughter of the deceased that this particular hymn most certainly would not do. "After all," he said with conviction, "this so-called hymn says nothing about community. In addition, and even worse," he went on, "it says not one word about God, Christ, or the Holy Spirit. Who is this person who 'Walks with me and talks with me?' Think about it. It doesn't say!' "

The bereaved daughter sat in surprised silence for a few minutes. Then she realized she was in no mood for a theology lesson or to explain to the pastor, whom she had never cared for in the first place, that everybody knew the hymn was about Jesus. She chose instead to guide him to the door. Thanking him for his trouble, she told him she had decided her mother's service would not take place in the church after all. The funeral home would be just fine and they could provide a pastor and an organist who would be happy to offer her the hymns of her choice. The church lost not only an elderly church member that week, but an entire family.

There is always a delicate balance for pastors between pleasing church members and being their teacher and guide in matters of faith. This book can obviously not advise about where each of its readers draws the boundaries of what music can and cannot be included in a service. We do want to meet people's needs and yet the church and pastor must maintain standards. The pastor in the above scenario might have agreed to the hymn "In the Garden" based on its history as a good old "war horse" from church music archives and its implication of Jesus. But what would he do when the next person asked to have someone sing "Memory" from *Cats?* You will have to use your own judgment, combined with the guidance of your area church body or denomination. Your church musician can help the family make appropriate choices. Remember, the families are often in too much pain to really know what they want. The service is always worship, so anything from your hymn book should be acceptable even if it may not be your personal favorite. If the music they want is truly secular, it might be possible to have it performed at the reception.

12

 reactions at the service

> Carol had been singing at funerals for a few years, but never one quite like this. She arrived at the church, took her place, and the service began. It was an elderly man who had died. His wife, his brother, and his sister were sitting together in the front row. The time came for Carol to sing the ever popular "Lord's Prayer" by Mallotte. About half way through her solo, the deceased's brother stood up, let out a loud anguished cry, and dropped to the floor. It seems he had suffered a heart attack. Now what?

There was a flurry. The pastor made some remarks about how the service would be postponed for a few minutes. Someone called 911. The ambulance arrived quickly, and the brother was taken out in a stretcher. Carol the soloist simply sat quietly and waited, wondering two things. First, was this brother going to survive? And, second, would she get her check? Finally, after some discussion with the family, the pastor came over to her and asked if she would please sing the song one more time? Carol obliged, but all the time thinking how strange it was that, after a man had nearly died during her song, they would even want to hear her sing again. Yes, she was paid, and she later was happy to receive a call that the brother had survived.

■ fainting

People react in different ways to grief. At any funeral service, or even at meetings you may have with the bereaved before or after the service, there is always the possibility that someone may faint. People rarely know in advance that they are about to pass out, so you will need to be ready to offer appropriate help. The person may become pale and, before you know it, have passed out on the floor. Catch them if you can, to prevent their falling, if you are the person closest. Then gently lead them to a comfortable place to sit and ask them to put their head down and just relax. If they have already fallen, don't expect them to jump up right away. It may be better that they wake up slowly. You will also have to decide if there could be other medical issues involved. Ask the closest family member if you should call a doctor. If the person does not wake up pretty quickly, call 911 and of course stay with the person until professional help arrives. And even if you don't know the person who fainted, be sure to take the time to follow up with a visit the next day, or at least a telephone call.

■ weeping

Although most people manage to contain their weeping even at funerals, you should be ready for the possibility that someone may cry out or weep so uncontrollably that your words cannot be heard. In this case, it might be best if you stop for just a minute or two — if you think the weeping will subside. If it looks like it will continue, go ahead gently or, in the most extreme situation, maybe even go over and embrace the person for a few seconds until they calm down. No one is to blame. It may be that your words have touched on certain memories. Or sometimes people have just come to the end of their tether and can't wait until they are alone, and they simply cry out. Sometimes they don't even realize they are the ones making the sounds. These situations are quite rare, but you should be prepared.

■ surprises

When it comes to funerals, pastors have to be ready for surprises. It is difficult to explain, but people in the early stages of deep grief sometimes say strange things, or do strange things. It is important that you do not overreact and that you try to understand.

SCENARIO _____

George was a beginner, doing a pastoral internship between his last two years of seminary. This was going to be his first funeral. He was nervous, but he was ready. He had written quite a fine funeral sermon. He was wearing his brand new pastoral robe. What could go wrong? He made his entrance with as much dignity as he could muster for the beginner he knew he was. There was the casket at the end of the center aisle. There was the wife and family of the deceased seated in the front pew. He found his way to the lectern and began to speak. No sooner had he started than the widow jumped from her seat and ran to the casket. She reached her arms in and actually yanked her dead husband's body upright, practically knocking it out of the casket. She wept loudly and cried out, "I love you. I love you." George stood in silent shock. The funeral home attendants rushed up to the widow, also trying their best to look calm. After what were probably only a few seconds, George pulled himself together and went to the widow, who by then had been separated from her husband's body, and the body returned to its place in the casket. The widow stood in embarrassed silence. George put his arm around her, and whispered "We understand. Yes, we understand," as he gently guided her back to her seat. Returning to the lectern, somehow he managed to compose himself and continue the service as if nothing at all had happened. George had experienced as a brand new pastor what we might call a "baptism by fire" into the ministry!

13

 ## options for exits

If the service is in a funeral home, when the service ends the funeral directors will come forward to make any announcements. These include telling the congregation that they are invited to follow the hearse in cars out to the cemetery. If this is not the case, they may announce that the family invites everyone to a reception to follow immediately in the church hall or at someone's home. In some funeral homes, the directors tend to slip away while the service is in progress and do not always return in time to make the announcements. It is a good idea for you to give them clear instructions on how long you expect the service to last and what words you will be saying as you complete the service. This way they will be there when you need them. If there are no funeral directors present, then it is your job to make the announcements. This is of course also the case if the service is at the church.

After these announcements, you may exit, but probably it is best to go directly to the family, embrace or shake hands as appropriate to your relationship with them, and then lead them out of the sanctuary. The congregation will follow. If the spouse is alone, you might take this person by the arm out to the narthex or hall. If the closest to the deceased (for example, the spouse) is already arm in arm with a family member or dear friend, then you can just lead them out.

14

 at the final resting place

■ the cortege to the place of burial or inurnment

It has been traditional for the entire entourage to drive in a long line out to the cemetery, with car lights on so that other drivers will recognize them as a funeral cortege and get out of the way. This would allow the long line of funeral cars to pass through all red lights and remain together. In years past, it was also customary for people walking in the area to remove their hats and stand in quiet respect as the cars passed en route to the cemetery. Nowadays, most walkers and drivers hardly even realize that a funeral cortege is passing.

Whatever car you drive, try to take your place in the line with as much dignity as your car will afford you. If the car is clean it is likely nobody will take offense. Your other option is to ride to the cemetery with the funeral directors in their car. They will always invite you. If you do go with them, you will have a chance to chat with them. The only negative about going in the funeral home car is that you will have to go back with them as well unless someone else offers to take you, and this may take quite a bit longer than you had planned.

■ at the cemetery or mausoleum

The rules are changing quickly in regard to farewells at the cemetery. For example, it is not uncommon for the reception to follow immediately after the service, and be held at church, funeral home, or restaurant, and then for the family to go out to say their cemetery farewells at some other time before or after the funeral and reception. Most often, at the cemetery, the pastor will offer some minimal leadership, gathering the people around the gravesite to offer a reading from scripture, a few words, and prayers.

Your words at the gravesite, memorial garden, or mausoleum should include words of commendation or committal — in which you commend or commit the deceased into the loving care of God. These words are intended to take place after the casket has been lowered (although the funeral home people now rarely lower the casket in the presence of the gathered group). You will say something like this. "Almighty God, we commend your servant Robert Jones into your loving care. Accept him now, a sheep of your fold, a lamb of your flock, a faithful and a good person." (You will have appropriate words in your own denominational books or traditions; this is just an example.) If there is no point after the service when you will be present for the body to be interred or the ashes laid or scattered, then it is appropriate for you to speak these words at the conclusion of the service, immediately before the benediction. If at the gravesite, you may wish to close with a benediction and then some kind of sending forth, such as "Go in peace," which signals the completion of the gravesite portion of the service and also lets the people know they may begin to speak with each other or leave.

In some families, the loved ones may wish to say a few words to the gathering at the cemetery. If possible, ascertain their interest in advance so you may adjust your words accordingly and also so you can announce that they will speak.

The length of time a family wishes to stay at the gravesite will vary widely. Sometimes it will be only five or ten minutes. Other families tend to linger, even after the pastor has gone. Whatever the family chooses is appropriate. Just be sure you check in with the close family to be sure they are ready for you to leave if you go before they do.

On occasion, you may be asked to place ashes or scatter ashes on a gravesite where a family member (usually a spouse) has already been buried. Be sure you know in advance which method of doing this is legal and accords with the rules of the cemetery. Also, ask the cemetery people or funeral home exactly what you will be expected to do. There may be a hole dug in advance in which you are to place an urn. Or you may simply be expected to set the urn on top of the grave of a family member, and then the cemetery people will place it in a hole after everyone has left. At times, you may be expected to actually scatter ashes over the grave. The volume of ashes can be quite large. You may find it difficult to spread them over one grave without covering the grave three or four times. It works well if you start pouring the ashes carefully, beginning close to the stone or monument and then moving in a swaying motion back and forth across the grave. If you get to the end of the grave and you still have ashes (and you probably will), then simply swing the open urn or bag of ashes slowly back and forth again, this time back toward the headstone. Repeat this motion until you run out of ashes. In the end, the grave will be covered in a blanket of ashes which will, in time, sink into the ground. A warning: keep the container low to the ground when you are doing this. Otherwise, if there is a breeze, the ashes could blow in the direction of the gathered people or land on other graves.

■ at the memorial garden

If the ashes of the deceased are being placed in your church's memorial garden, then it is likely, although not always the fact, that the entire congregation will be following you out to the garden at the conclusion of the service. It is good if you can get a deacon or elder to assist you in this short walk to the garden and after you get there. You will need to bring the box or urn of ashes, which can be heavy. You will also be carrying your notes in a book or small binder and usually also a Bible or Psalm book. The hole will have been dug in advance, and it is most often you, the pastor, who have had to arrange for this, even if it is done through your memorial garden committee. You don't want to lead the group or family out to the garden only to find that there is no hole dug where the ashes can be placed.

When you arrive at the location where the hole has been dug, wait till all are present. Then ask them to make a semicircle around you so that everyone can see and hear. If any family members or guests cannot stand for long, make advance arrangements for folding chairs or some other kind of seating for them.

Once the group is settled, it is time to begin. It is good if you can find a gracious way to tell them you will only be saying a few words, especially if the weather is bad. Then proceed. If you have not read Psalm 23, this is a good time to do so. Also, you may say you are pouring the ashes into the ground and placing the deceased into the tender care of Almighty God. You may have a short prayer at the beginning, at the end, or both. You will then place the ashes into the hole or scatter them. The way that you do this will depend on the traditions of your area and also on any laws or regulations of your town, city, or county. For example, in some areas with high water tables, the ashes must be placed in the ground without being in any kind of containers, including even plastic bags. In other locations, it is perfectly acceptable to put the ashes into the ground in an urn, a box, or a bag. Be sure you are aware of the local regulations. The funeral home people should be able to tell you. They will also help explain this to the family.

If it is raining, you may be able to postpone the memorial garden portion of the service until another day. But if it is decided that you will go ahead in the rain, you will definitely require a helper to hold an umbrella over you, and have umbrellas handy for the immediate family. You'll need to keep your hands free to pour the ashes and also to hold any notes or your Bible, keeping them from getting wet. It is very difficult to keep the rain off your papers. To pour the loose ashes into the hole with as much dignity as you can in the rain, it helps to have some kind of simple but attractive cover placed over the hole in advance. It might be made of wood or tile. That way there will not be any rainwater getting into the hole. You might also arrange for a basket to be placed near the hole, containing some earth and a small garden spade (covered with strong plastic if it is raining). After you have spoken words of consolation to the gathered group, you can hand your book to the deacon, elder, or funeral home representative, place the ashes in the hole, then pick up the spade and drop some earth in over the ashes. After this has been done, you will complete the ritual with a few more words, a closing prayer, and benediction. Tell the people the service is ended, but that they may stay longer if they wish. Then your deacon, elder, or funeral home representative will place the cover back over the hole and all will depart. Shortly after, when all have left, have the deacon or elder return, fill the hole up to the top with earth, pat it down firmly, and remove the cover and basket to be used again.

15

 ## a dinner or reception following the service

For reasons including those that follow, it is a very good idea for you to be present at funeral receptions, whether they are taking place in your church hall or elsewhere.

■ theological purpose of the reception

It may seem strange at first to think of the reception, a social event, as having profound theological significance. Yet it is at this reception that the family and friends begin to regroup. The deceased takes a new position in the family in that this person becomes a memory, a remembered person, while others move into new positions. It is much like a mobile of glass pieces hanging from the ceiling; when one piece is removed, every other piece shifts to another position. Jobs and responsibilities that the deceased had in the family will be passed on to other people. Leadership will change and roles will shift. The mobile will continue to hang and it will still be beautiful, but it will be different, never the same again. Graydon Snyder and I describe it this way: "Stories are told that recall the joy and happy memories of the one who has died. There is laughter and happiness. Resurrection occurs. Sins are forgotten or disappear. Enemies forgive and are forgiven. There is new life in the community. There is enough food for everyone and for others who might be in need or cannot be present. As they sit at tables together the family reorganizes itself. Perhaps even the faith community will do the same. We call it resurrection."*

■ your pastoral purposes for being there

The family and others will continue to need your support at any reception that follows the service. The immediate family will be spending this time greeting those who have attended the service, seeing who has come, renewing old acquaintances, and having a chance to mingle with the people who cared enough to come. At times, you will be able to actually observe how the grieving takes a turn to a real sense of celebration of the life of the deceased. People will gather in small groups, often remembering and speaking fondly of the deceased. There will often be smiling, even laughter. Sometimes new configurations of family and even of friends will show their beginnings at this reception.

As the pastor, you probably won't even have to decide what group or person to go and speak with. People will usually make

---

*Graydon Snyder and Doreen McFarlane, *The People Are Holy: The History and Theology of Free Church Worship* (Macon, GA: Mercer University Press, 2005), 110.

their way to you. They may tell you what a meaningful service this was for them. This is their way of opening conversation. They often want to tell you about their personal relationship with the deceased, especially if they shared some good life experiences. There are times too that someone will seek you out at a reception such as this and really be at some stage of being a "seeker." The person may have been away from church for a long time and now has had a good church experience and hopes you will be kind. These are the opportunities to be sensitive to their needs. They may never show up at your church door again, but still may have been moved one step closer to a relationship with their creator because you were good to them on this day of sadness.

■ reception in your church hall — your role as host

If the reception is being held in your church hall, you are to some degree also a host to all who have come. If the women (or men) of the church are providing the refreshments, then you are also present in some capacity for them. After you visit with the guests and perhaps join them for a cup of coffee, you might want to also spend some time with your church members who prepared the refreshments. They will be staying for quite a while to clean up after the event, and they are nearly always volunteers as members of some kind of hospitality or social committee. They appreciate the pastor's seeing the work they are doing for their beloved church.

We have walked our way through the day of the service. Now you are ready. But, as we pastors all know, there are exceptions to every rule. Part 3 will address a variety of special circumstances for funerals.

part three

special circumstances

16

 ## funerals of gay or lesbian persons

■ like any other funerals

Everything in this book applies equally to a service for a gay or lesbian person. So why a special section for gays and lesbians? It is only included so that you, the pastor, can be especially sensitive to issues that you may not have dealt with before. First you will need to know if the deceased was openly gay or lesbian, and if this person had made known his or her wishes regarding whether this was to be openly spoken about at the service. Just because a parishioner was "out" to you does not mean he or she had also told family, friends, and fellow church members. You will be able to determine best from conversation with the loved ones how you might approach this aspect of the person's identity and life.

■ respecting the beloved partner or spouse

It is important to show particular care toward the beloved partner of the deceased. There are situations in which any living
parents are not in rapport with the partner and when both will
feel strongly that they are the primary "family member." You
will have to be sensitive to all parties concerned and try to determine what the deceased would have wanted. Of course, the law
will determine which are legally the primary family members.
As gay and lesbian marriages are now being recognized in many
states, this will become less of an issue.

■ engaging the new traditional language

You and the loved ones can best determine what words to use to
describe the deceased person's partner: "life-partner," "spouse,"
"wife," or "husband"?

■ dealing with family members who do not (yet) understand

There will be family members and also acquaintances and friends
at the service who really do not understand why this person was
gay or lesbian. They may even openly disapprove of your open-
ness toward them or try to "remind" you of theological stances
on the issue that they believe to be true. Do not attempt to engage with them on the matter. A funeral is not an appropriate
place for this discussion. They have already experienced your
response to the deceased and partner or family as a positive one.
Your role-modeling is message enough about how you feel. If
they really push you, you might make an appointment with them
to talk about it in another setting. The funeral is a time to remember and celebrate the life of the deceased. It is not a forum
for debating theological differences.

■ the rewards of officiating at a gay or lesbian person's funeral

As more and more states and countries in the world accept gay and lesbian marriages, perhaps with time the matter will no longer be contentious. Today, some pastors may still have a sense of trepidation about officiating at a funeral service for a lesbian or gay person. If you really feel uncomfortable about doing it, then help the family to find someone else to do it. It is better that they be served by a pastor who accepts them for who they are than to have an uncertain person in leadership. If you do go ahead, and let's hope that you do, you may be surprised. Your work will be deeply appreciated and you will know, in your heart, that you did the right thing.

17

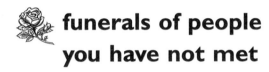 funerals of people you have not met

SCENARIO _____

Linda was a busy new church pastor. She was on the run from morning till night, rushing around trying to care for her family and church members. She was always worried about not getting enough people to join the new congregation she served. Recently, she had met a nice young woman and the woman had attended worship twice. She hoped this young woman and her family would decide to join the church. The young woman's father died, and Linda thought it would be good to attend the service, even though she had never met the father. She headed out the door that day, in her usual rush, driving as fast as she could to the funeral home. She dashed in and sat down. As soon as she got settled, the service began. A Lutheran pastor? How strange. She was quite sure the young woman had told her that her dad was a Baptist. Wait a minute! Where was that young woman anyway? Linda sat through about ten minutes of the service before it hit her that she was at the wrong funeral! In her hurry to be on time, she'd walked right into the wrong chapel at the funeral home, without even looking at the name on the board. She felt even more embarrassed when she realized people were beginning to turn heads and stare at her, surely wondering who on earth she was! When the service ended, she headed for the guest book, wrote in her name with the title Reverend, and quickly left. This way, family members would at least know the strange unknown woman at the funeral was a pastor. She headed for the door and decided she'd do better in the future to take things just a bit slower. She never did get to the funeral she had been heading for. And she was too ashamed to tell her prospective new member that she had at least tried to attend her father's funeral.

The day comes for almost every pastor when that call comes from the local funeral director with a request to perform a service (usually at the funeral home or at a gravesite) for a person that pastor has never met. There is, of course, no requirement that you accept. If you have associates or assistants, or neighboring ministerial colleagues who are known to do such services, you might suggest that one of them take the service. They often have more time and are glad for the experience. But if this is not an option, you might want to say yes. Your pastoral instincts are calling you to help those in need. The fact that someone who has left this world needs you now is very compelling. So you say yes and somehow manage to fit it into your busy schedule. God bless you for doing this. It is a service not only to the deceased and any relatives or friends but also to the community.

It may surprise you that certain members of the church you currently serve may seem a bit disconcerted about your decision. They may be thinking (although not saying) that you are bought and paid for by them. If they ask why you are doing this for a stranger, you can always explain your willingness to provide a needed service to the community and a gesture of God's hospitality to the stranger.

Once you accept, it is time to spring into action. While you are on the phone with the funeral home people, ask them these questions:

• When is the obituary coming and out and can they send or email a copy to you? What are the names and phone numbers of the immediate family members? When would be a good time to contact them?

• Is there anything they can tell you about the deceased and about the family?

• Did the deceased have any church or religious affiliation at all? This will help you to formulate the style of service and the wording of your prayers and sermon.

Now call the closest family member and have a list of questions prepared in advance. This way you can take notes easily while speaking. Unless they are so distraught they can't speak with you, they are likely to be anxious to tell you about their loved one. Make them feel comfortable about the fact that, even though you do not know each other, you are calling to comfort them and you are honored to do the service. They are often very grateful for this and anxious to connect with you as clergy. Here is a short list of things you might say and ask:

• Introduce yourself and say how sorry you are to hear of their loss of the loved one.

• Explain that you are calling to get some information so that the service will be more meaningful to them.

• Get a good clear list of the family members whose names you will mention at the service. Later you can cross-check this with the obituary. After they give you the list of names, be sure to ask if there is anyone else who may not have been mentioned. You will be surprised how many times they come up with another name of a sibling or close relative who has been estranged.

The next thing you do is the most important.

- Simply say, "Tell me about your husband/wife/sister." They nearly always will tell you everything you need to know and more. If you don't feel you are getting enough information to put together a decent service in this person's honor, then you might also speak to other members of the family who are available. If someone deemed important by the family has not arrived yet, you can have them call you later.

- Try to steer them away from only talking about the illness and death (which of course is primary on their minds) and move to questions about the past. If you happen to get someone who is not offering any real information, then you can ask such things as: "Did he like sports?" "Did she enjoy her work?" "Did he have any hobbies?" "What about travel?" Try to determine what is important to share about their deceased loved one, and then sit down and put together a simple but respectable service.

- You may want to check to see if the family would like to have someone else give a eulogy. This is becoming more and more common and adds a very personal touch to the service. Do try to keep the family from making the service into a major production. A longer service is not necessarily a better one. Your good judgment will be relied upon, and you will be held responsible.

In the end, it is really satisfying when you hear these words from people after the service "I know you didn't know my dad (uncle, friend) but you really captured the essence of him. I don't know how you did it but thanks. It meant a lot to all of us!"

18

 funerals for elderly people

The funeral home people called Pastor John and arranged for him to officiate at a service for a woman named Maizie, who had lived to the grand age of ninety-six. Pastor John was told they had not been able to reach any family members but that the service had been paid for in advance; in fact, the deceased had paid in full, herself, over twenty years earlier, when she thought she was getting old at the age of seventy-six. She had even written a few words at that time for her obituary. Pastor John didn't know what her life had been since that time, but he put together a few nice words from what little information he had, and, when the day came, he arrived to perform the service.

There Maizie lay, in the casket that she herself had ordered and paid for all those years before. Pastor John robed up and waited at the entrance of the chapel. The time arrived for the service but nobody came in. He waited ten more minutes and not one person showed up. It seemed that this dear woman had outlived not only her family but all her friends as well. It would have been so easy for John to simply take off his robe and head for home. Instead, he made a decision. He strode into the funeral home offices where four people were working, and said: "I'm putting on a funeral here. It appears nobody is coming to the service. I am planning to go ahead anyway. I think Miss Maizie would appreciate it if one or two of you would come into the chapel and help me give her a nice send-off. What do you say?" Out of the four in that office, three got up from their desks and walked in to attend the service. It was short but grand. The funeral home people seemed pleased. And the angels were surely smiling!

When you perform a service for a person who has lived to a really ripe old age, it is good if you can speak with people who have known the person at different times of life. The reason is that, even though people may not change dramatically, there are likely to be people at the service who knew the deceased in different ways. For example, the experience of a spouse will likely cover a long span of years. Still, once the spouse has gotten over telling you details about the illness and death, it is very likely that the stories will include sweeter memories of youth, struggles as a young couple, and long past days of happiness. The children of the deceased often present a very different picture. To them, the deceased was always an "older" person and they will speak often of travels they took with their parents when they were children, of advice they received from the deceased, or of time the parent took to pay attention to their needs as young people. Siblings will often speak of the childhood they shared with the deceased and are sometimes known to carry their childhood opinions of the person throughout their lives. Also, the memories of each individual sibling may vary widely.

No matter how old the person lived to be, loved ones are apt still to be shocked at their passing. In many families, there has never been a thought or a word about the impending death, even as aging people go through illness after serious illness. In these cases, there is no purpose served in pointing out to the loved ones that this person's lifespan had simply come to an end. Still, you can mention somewhere in the service the fact that this person lived "a long and fruitful life."

19

 funerals for those
with premature deaths

■ for those who have committed suicide

The death of a loved one by suicide is particularly heartbreaking. It is difficult enough when one has died of natural causes or even from an accident. The person who has taken his or her own life has made a choice not to go on living. For whatever reason, known or unknown to the family, this person has found it so unbearable to continue living that he or she chose death instead.

Close family members left to mourn may be suffering deeply from a wide range of emotions. One is guilt; they may feel somehow responsible for the death, a nearly always unfounded but very real emotion. Or family members may be secretly experiencing anger at the deceased for leaving them, but feeling unable or unwilling to voice this anger. You, as the pastor, may be the only "safe" person who can listen to these emotions, should the person even be able to articulate them. In addition, there are emotions that are impossible to express. All this, in addition to the socially unspoken but still present stigma against suicide can make suicide an embarrassment for some family members. Your work as a pastor and caregiver will not be easy.

To begin, it will be important for you to know whether the cause of death by suicide is public knowledge, known by family members only, or by a few. You don't want to be the one who blurts out this information. On the other hand, if it is generally known, you will want to address it in some way in the service. Otherwise, it will look like you're trying to keep it quiet. Let the family lead the way in this regard as you prepare for the service.

Suicide has been considered to be a soul-threatening taboo in some church traditions. In others, it has been long understood as an illness or, at least, a forgivable action on the part of a deeply troubled person. As the pastor, you represent not only yourself when you speak, but also your church's teachings. If you find yourself, for any reason, unable to perform the service in a way that is life-sustaining to the family, then it is best that you gracefully help them find someone else who can lead the service. In some cases, there is a delicate balance between speaking the "word" of your denomination's stance on an issue as promised in your ordination, and the "words" that will help a grieving family.

Suicide devastates not only the family but every individual who cared for the one who has died. Emotions will be running deep through the entire gathered congregation. When hearts are breaking, God's message of forgiveness and Jesus' words of love are needed more than ever. You are called and privileged to speak them.

Families of those who die by suicide will probably need counseling over time, and most often it is best given from a professional counselor. They will need you too as their pastor to watch and care for them over time.

■ for small children (or other young people)

Nothing is more difficult for a pastor than to be called to officiate at a service for a baby, a child, or a young adult. There is often the element of shock for the parents, as well as for family and friends. A deep sadness seems to fill everyone who even hears of such a death. For those closest to the person, the pain can be overwhelming.

Your pastoral care of the people closest to the deceased will have to be particularly sensitive. You will need to offer both immediate care and continuing support. Divorces are very common among couples following the loss of their child. One reason is that the stages of grief find their way to people at different times and in different ways. Each member of the couple (the parents) will likely be going through these stages of grief at a different time from the other. It is quite possible (unless you are a specially trained grief counselor) that the family will need professional help in addition to any that you offer as their pastor.

The biggest issue for you is that you take care not to say the wrong thing. It is better to stand by in silence than to say something that could cause further pain to the family. General ideas about death and dying may be fine for discussion groups but, in the throes of the horrendous grieving of the loss of a child, *do not say:* "God needed her more than you did" or "God must have had a reason. God's ways are not our ways." (This may be true but it is no consolation and only brings feelings of anger toward God.)

Another expression of sympathy that may or may not be acceptable to a grieving parent is "She is out of her pain now." This may be true — but why not out of pain and also alive? A touch of the hand, a pat on the back, or sincere eye contact may be the very best prayers you can give.

Now when it comes to the service, you will have no choice but to speak. In recent years, pastors have learned that it is all right to say something like this: "We don't know why such a senseless thing has happened. We can only live in the promises of God that things will be made right in the end, and, as it says in the Book of Revelation, 'God will wipe every tear from their eyes.' " You will be able to speak good things about this young person and about the joy the person brought to others in his or her short life.

When a teenager or young adult dies, you may find yourself surrounded by this person's friends. They often stand vigil at the hospital before the death, at the wake or calling hours, and come in groups to the service. They may be exceedingly emotional, tearful, and also talkative. These young people are generally not only dealing with the death of their friend. They are also facing, many of them for the first time, the fact that life is not always fair and that death is a reality. At the service, some may even be experiencing their first time at worship. Be especially sensitive to their presence and their suffering. Their suffering may seem overly dramatic at times, but it is very real.

■ for those who have died in accidents

Accidental deaths are a huge shock for everyone who is left. If the deceased is a member of your church and a friend, you too will be in some grief of your own. Always try to be aware of your own emotions in relation to a funeral you will lead. You can think you are being objective and pastoral, but there are times in your ministry when you are much more deeply involved emotionally than you realize.

When people die in accidents, it is very often the case that they have not died with their papers in order or any funeral plans lined up. So the combination of being shocked by the death and also having to deal with issues of finances, distribution of belongings, and perhaps surviving children who need care can make it very difficult for immediate family members. You may, for this reason, find them somewhat distracted when you are trying to make the funeral plans together. It will be good if you can help them focus on the task at hand. They may also ask you to assist them in solving any number of issues related to the death. Keep clearly in mind which jobs and what specific matters of problem solving are your business and which are not.

Another matter related to accidental death is that there may be more than one person who has died. In such cases, be sure to take time for each of the deceased, even if they are all members of the same family, rather than grouping them together for all your remarks. There will be people at the service who are mainly there for one of the deceased and will need to hear you speak about that person. In a case where more than one family member has died, the rest of the family will be even more devastated. Your work will be difficult. But in such cases of multiple death it is likely that church members and friends of the family will come forward to help.

A voice says, "Cry out!":
And I said, "What shall I cry?"
All people are grass.
The grass withers, the flower fades,
when the breath of the Lord blows upon it;
Surely the people are grass.
The grass withers, the flower fades;
but the word of our God will stand forever.

(Isa. 40:6–8)

All of us find it difficult to confront our mortality. That everyone — and that we — will die is what we cannot face easily. Our society today seems to conspire to keep us from facing or talking about the fact that we all will die. Yet death touches every family, sometimes sooner and sometimes later. This scripture passage from Isaiah reflects the fact that, although all human beings will die, God's word will never pass away. Ancient Hebrews, even though their faith did not necessarily include belief in a specific heavenly afterlife, still put all their trust and all their hope in the word of God. We can learn from them of the value of living every day to its fullest to the glory of the God who gave the gift of life.

■ for those who die after lifelong illnesses

It is very sad when a person has had an entire lifetime of serious illness. Such a person has lived but missed enjoying good health and many of the joys of living. It is important that you address this at the funeral rather than making excuses or pretending everything was all right. Everyone at the funeral will know about the long illness and the family will have suffered in relation to this illness as well.

Sometimes people will suggest that the person's illness was so devastating that the life would have been better not to have been at all. This is seldom, if ever, the case. All people, however devastating their disability, experience some human joys and possess some talent and ability. Perhaps it was as simple as the fact that they tried their best or they could make someone smile. The family members — particularly those who lived with or cared for the deceased — will tell you what the person's attributes were if you do not know them yourself.

■ for those who have been murdered

It may seem that murder occurs so seldom that there is no need to address it in a book such as this. Still, when it does, the pastor is caught unawares, being expected to know what to do and say, and wanting to prepare and lead a service that will bring consolation and God's love to a devastated family.

Some people are murdered because they are hated; many because they are "loved" too much. Some are murdered simply because they were in the wrong place at the wrong time. Some are murdered protecting others in the line of duty; others involved in illegal activities. Whatever the reason, death was not the choice of the person who died. Every family member will be in deep shock, each probably in a different stage of grief. There will be anger directed at the murderer, known or unknown, and sometimes also toward others, even self or fellow family members for not having done something to prevent the tragedy. Although any long-term counseling of the family will not likely be up to you, you will have some responsibility to get them through the service.

What words can you offer at such a service? Remember that it is not the family's responsibility to punish the killer. The police will do their best and, as hard as this may be to accept, the rest is up to God. "Vengeance is mine, says the Lord" (Rom. 12:19). The funeral service is not the place for any talk about the murderer because, like any other funeral, it must focus on the deceased.

When you sit with family members to plan the service, get them to talk about the good things about their loved one. This will help to get their minds off the shock and be a very initial opening for what will be a long, slow healing process. At the service, it is best not to dwell on the deceased's potential and aspirations that will never be realized. Concentrate, rather, on the gift their life has been to those who knew and loved them and on the fact that none of us knows the hour or the day that death will come. Even though it is generally a good idea to invite others to speak at funerals, it might not be so good in the case of a murdered person. The talk could easily turn to a polemic on violence, an uncontrolled emotional outburst, or even an accusation against a suspect that could bring on a suit for defamation of character. It is much safer for the family to share their thoughts with you and have you, as pastor, be the speaker.

In some cases, the murderer is known or suspected but, for some legal reason has not been apprehended. It is even possible that the murderer will show up at the service, in a low key but public display of innocence and grief. What will you say if the family requests that you ask the person to leave? The police are also likely to be at the funeral, observing. The best thing for you to do is graciously deny the family's request, reminding them that this is a police matter and your asking the person to leave might interfere with their work. Again, help the family to focus on the deceased and not on the suspect.

■ miscarriage/reproductive loss

In the past, the death of a baby before taking the first breath was often pushed aside. Parents were left to grieve alone, as society and even the clergy suggested they simply move on and that things should go better in the next pregnancy.

As a pastor, what can you do to alleviate the suffering women or couples and their families? It will be necessary for them to take the lead. Be available to them, possibly by means of a hospital or home visit. You should get a sense of what they might need, and then only can you make suggestions. In many cases, the visit will have done them good, offering them a chance to share their feelings with someone they trust. Other times they may want or need some kind of service to take place. This could be between you and the immediate family only, or with a few invited close friends. It could take place at hospital, home, or church. The service might be short but somewhat formal if that seems appropriate for the loved ones. Like any funeral, it would include prayers, scripture reading, and a few words from you or a chosen family representative about how the child is now safely in the loving care of God. Your words should acknowledge the loss, and express words of hope as well, to offer encouragement.

In some cases, parents will request that the deceased baby be baptized. This presents a dilemma for some pastors whose church's teachings may suggest or insist that only the living are in need of baptism. Still, if you are given any flexibility in this regard, err on the side of grace for the sake of the grieving parents. Some people secretly worry that their child is not welcome in heaven if not baptized. You personally may believe that baptism is neither appropriate nor necessary for a deceased or stillborn child, but if you can bring consolation to suffering parents, the baptism is an act of love and compassion. You will have to make arrangements with the hospital staff to go to the child. The parents may or may not be present, as they choose. For baptism, of course the only necessary elements are water and "the word."

20

 funerals for military persons

■ military honors

Officially, military honors include flag folding, flag presentation, and the playing of Taps. Although Taps is officially to be played by a bugler, due to shortage of buglers, the military sometimes offers a tape or CD of Taps. If the family tells you they want military honors, have them ask the funeral directors who will then contact the appropriate military service. It should be a person from the veteran's parent Service who comes to present the flag. If a bereaved family makes the request, military honors can sometimes also include a gun salute at the cemetery or memorial garden. In some cases, the military will send a group (usually veterans) under the leadership of one appointed leader. These people do not come to be part of the congregation at the funeral service. They are usually posted at some short distance at the time you arrive at the cemetery. Their leader will stay in touch with you. It is good if you have a few minutes to go over and speak with the leader and thank them in advance. That way, you and the leader can coordinate the timing of the gun salute, which should take place at the conclusion of your words at the cemetery. The leader will then present the nearest family member with a folded flag, speaking a few words privately to that person about the country's appreciating the loved one's military service. You can make a short announcement, perhaps: "The family will now be presented with the flag, in honor of their loved one's military service."

For information about eligibility for military honors, here are two websites currently active:

www.militaryfuneralhonors.oc.mil, sponsored by the Department of Defense

www.military.com, sponsored by the National Guard.

■ for veterans of World War II, the Korean War, or the Vietnam War

It is important that you check with the family about whether the deceased was a veteran. It happens more often than one might guess that a spouse or family forgets to even mention that the deceased was in the service. There have been times that I found out quite by accident that the deceased was a veteran and, in more than one case, even a war hero. So don't forget to ask: "Was he (or she) by any chance in the armed forces?" This way, if they do tell you about or show you any medals or honors the person received, you will be able to speak of this in the funeral service. In addition, all U.S. veterans are entitled to the presentation of a folded flag, either at the close of the service or at the conclusion of your words at the cemetery (as mentioned in the previous section).

■ for those who have died serving in the Middle East

With the rising number of deaths of military personnel serving in Iraq and Afghanistan and related service, it is necessary to address here the possibility that you might be called to perform a service for a military person who had been on active duty there. You will be deeply saddened by this untimely death, especially if the deceased was a member of your church. This will make it even harder for you than many other funerals. Even if you did not know the deceased well, you will be in grief over the loss of a young, healthy, and dedicated public servant who was willing to be in harm's way for love of country.

You may harbor negative feelings or even have openly spoken against war in general, or against this war in particular. Of course, the funeral is not an appropriate place to bring up these issues. The deceased has made his or her choices in this respect and these are to be honored. In addition, pride in the military service of the deceased may be helping the family to cope in these early days of grief. If you feel so strongly about the matter that you do not think you can honor the military service of the deceased, you might consider asking an associate or other pastor to officiate at the service. On the other hand, if the family is expecting you, it should be you if at all possible. You can certainly honor the life of a service person without glorifying war.

You can expect a large gathering

In addition to family, friends, and church members, it is likely that members of the larger community will want to pay their respects at the funeral of a veteran. If the family expects the numbers to be overwhelming, they can request a private service or a service by invitation only. It might be possible to invite the community to come only to the cemetery, or to gather at some other location to remember and mourn, either while the service takes place or at a later time.

You can expect a heartbroken family

Military families are expected to understand that death in the line of duty may be the result of the military service of their loved one. Still, it is always a shock. The loved ones will be heartbroken but may also have a justified sense of pride in the courage and selflessness their military person has exhibited. Each member of the family will react differently.

There is often a spouse and small children

Perhaps the worst-case scenario for a military death is the one in which the deceased leaves a spouse and small children. The spouse will know best whether the children should attend the funeral and this will also depend on their ages. At this time, your skills in pastoral care will be especially needed. A military chaplain may also be assigned to the family and this person might be able to help a lot. Be open to receiving this person's assistance. It may also be a good plan for the family to get some ongoing professional counseling.

Military honors

The deceased will, of course, receive full military honors. The person's parent Service will very likely guide you in any form of military protocol expected at the service.

21

 funerals in which the
deceased and the family
are of different faiths

Where you go, I will go.
Where you lodge, I will lodge.
Your people shall be my people,
and your God my God.
Where you die, I will die —
and there will I be buried.

(Ruth 1:16b–17a)

When two people are truly committed to each other, it is not
uncommon for one to embrace the faith of the other and even
ask to be buried in a gravesite of the other's faith community.
It is most often a husband and wife but sometimes between
people in some other adoptive type family relationship. The
person's request is sincere and should be respected.

Sometimes the deceased and family are of different faiths or denominations. The deceased, for example, may be a Protestant
and most or all of the family Roman Catholic. The Protestant
pastor will be responsible to perform a service that is authentic to
the deceased's faith stance, while also welcoming and comforting
the family members who are of a different faith. In cases such as
these, you may have to ask questions of the family about their
needs. You also may need to take extra time to explain things
you will be doing that are rituals or practices of your faith but
not of theirs.

Sometimes a situation will arise in which the deceased was very religious but the family is agnostic. In these cases, it is good to speak about the person's faith and devotion to God. Do not avoid it because you think it will not be important to the family. Friends and church members will want and need to have you speak about the person's faith.

There are also situations that are the opposite. For example, the deceased may not have been religious at all but the spouse or family members are. They may ask you to say things that do not authentically describe the deceased. Show them respect, but don't let them set the agenda in a way that does not seem right. Friends and acquaintances attending the service are likely to know if your words do not reflect the genuine personality of the deceased.

You are responsible to the memory of the deceased and also to the family engaging you to lead the service. Look for words that will honor the deceased while also bringing comfort to those who live on.

22

 funerals in which some
are challenged

■ The deaf and the hard of hearing

If the deceased was a deaf person, it is likely there will be deaf friends attending the service. It is also possible, of course, that a deceased hearing person had deaf friends. If either is the case, you will have to do a little extra work. Have the family, if they wish, arrange for an ASL interpreter (American Sign Language). That person will need a copy of your words in advance of the service. At the service, she or he will require a clear sight line to you. Then, also, leave a cordoned off area in the sanctuary or chapel for deaf visitors who wish to sit there, so they can clearly see both you and the interpreter.

If you know some who are hard of hearing will be attending, be sure any hearing aid devices are clean and set out where they can be picked up and operated conveniently. It is also important that you speak clearly and not too quickly, because many listeners, especially older ones, choose not to use a hearing device.

■ the blind and the sight impaired

Strange as it may sound, be sure to give blind persons good seats, close to the front, unless they request otherwise. The reason is that many legally blind people are not totally blind, and they will appreciate being seated where they can see as best they can.

■ the mentally challenged

If a close family member is mentally challenged or if you are told there will be mentally challenged people attending the service, you may want to check over the service you are planning to see if you could say the same things in simpler or clearer — but no less beautiful or profound — language. The truth is that everyone appreciates clarity.

■ the physically challenged

Be sure to let family members know whether your church is handicapped accessible. If it is not so yet, your church may still be usable by people with wheelchairs, if you make a few advance arrangements and adjustments. Sometimes small temporary ramps can be put in. Family members can be assigned to lift wheelchairs if it is only up or down three or four steps. They can also assist people in getting in and out of bathrooms. Another room or a chapel might even be used for the service rather than the main sanctuary, if it is more accessible, perhaps from another door. Be creative.

This situation might also afford you a good opening with your church council or trustees to bring up the issue of making your facility handicapped accessible. A real-life example is always good to spur committees on to making good decisions.

23

 ## funerals when the spouse is estranged or divorced

It is not uncommon to perform a funeral in which the deceased has either been divorced or estranged from the spouse and had not remarried. In the case of divorce, the next of kin will then be the children if there are any, or siblings or parents. Occasionally the ex-spouse will have a part in the service, but is still not legally considered next of kin. In the case of estrangement, it depends on whether there was a legal separation. The funeral director will be able to give you the names of the official next of kin who are "putting on" the funeral. Be sure you are dealing with the right people to avoid any disagreement or conflict regarding details of the service. If the deceased was a member of your church, you are possibly also pastor to the estranged or divorced spouse (although it is common for at least one to change churches at the time of a separation). If you are pastor to both, you will need to be especially sensitive because you are serving both the estranged spouse and the family of the deceased. If they have children together, the children and the spouse are likely to be going through very different emotions. The spouse may exhibit a range of feelings, anything from ambiguity to intense dislike, or possibly love. The children may feel great love for the deceased, or they might be angry over their parents' separation. Don't be surprised that, on occasion, parents of divorced people may stay very close to both the husband and the wife. Take your cues from the immediate (official) family. And try to be sensitive to everyone. There are some divorces and estrangements that should never have happened in the first place. Sometimes the love between ex-spouses remains strong. Sometimes they had become good friends, often because of their children.

If the deceased was remarried, you probably will have little or no contact with the ex-spouse. Still, be sure to ask as diplomatically as you can if the first spouse should be listed among the names you read aloud during the service. If the first spouse was married to the deceased for many years and they raised children together, it can be entirely appropriate to include this name. Let the current spouse decide, possibly along with the children.

24

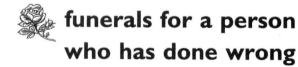 funerals for a person
who has done wrong

THEOLOGICAL REFLECTION _____

> *Then he [the criminal] said, "Jesus, remember me when you come into your kingdom." He replied "Truly I tell you, today you will be with me in Paradise."* (Luke 23:42–43)

Jesus does not speak one word of judgment against the criminals on his right and on his left, as he hangs suffering on the cross. Instead, according to the Gospel of Luke, Jesus gives the guarantee to the one to whom he is speaking that they will be "together" in Paradise. What grace! What forgiveness! What love!

Occasionally a pastor is asked to perform a service for someone who has committed a serious crime, or someone who is openly known to be a cheater, or a cruel or unkind person. This puts you in a really uncomfortable position. Your customary words of praise in remembrance of the deceased probably will not work here. It is important that you be honest. Still, you are not being engaged to speak against the person. The purpose of the service you perform is to bring consolation to the family members and friends who come to mourn or who attend out of a sense of obligation.

That said, what do you say? What can you say? Of course, it depends to some extent on what the person has done and how publicly this is known. You might be able to focus on some good qualities the person did possess. He or she may, for example, have done many bad things but, at the same time, always lovingly cared for a particular sibling, parent, or friend. The person may have suffered mental illness or bad treatment over the years as a child, which led to the bad behavior. You will not be making excuses when you speak of these things; rather, you are facing the fact that there are sometimes reasons why people choose to act in socially unacceptable ways.

Another option to deflect from focusing on the bad reputation of the deceased is to concentrate instead on the incredible grace of God. We are called not to judge people, as judgment is the work of God and not humans. God's forgiveness is unfathomable. This can bring consolation and hope.

One scripture verse that could be appropriate for such a funeral is Romans 8:35: "Who will separate us from the love of Christ? Will hardship, or distress, or persecution, or famine, or nakedness, or peril or sword?" And also verses that follow shortly after. "No, in all these things we are more than conquerors through him who loved us. For I am convinced that neither death, nor life, nor angels, nor rulers, nor things present, nor things to come, nor powers, nor height, nor depth, nor anything else in all creation, will be able to separate us from the love of God in Christ Jesus our Lord" (Rom. 8:37–39).

25

 funerals outside your church building

The church is the most appropriate venue for a Christian funeral service. Still, there are any number of places where such a service might take place and many reasons for this.

■ in a funeral home/parlor

You may be a pastor who regularly officiates at services at the local funeral homes — in which case you may not need to read this section. If, on the other hand, you do most of your funeral services at church, or you are in a city where there are multiple funeral homes, these tips might be helpful.

If you have not officiated at a service in a particular funeral home before, it is best if you can go there for a few minutes on the day before the service, or at least arrive a bit early just to check things out. This way, you will be more comfortable when the time comes to do the service. Introduce yourself to the funeral home people and ask them a few questions:

- Will there be piped in music? Will they be sure to turn it off when the service begins?

- Will they come in and close the casket before the service begins? (It is preferable in most cultures that it be closed at that time.)

- Will they escort you into the chapel for the service or, at the very least, let you know when to enter?

- Will they remain during the service? It is good if they can do this, so that when you are finished speaking they can come forward with any announcements.

- Will they make the announcement about travel to the cemetery and also about any reception or dinner to follow the service or do they expect you to do that?

You will also want to take a good look at the lectern. If it is not the appropriate height for you, can it be raised or lowered? Does it have proper lighting over your pages? If so, take a close look at how it can be switched on and off so that you don't fumble during the service. Funeral chapels often have subdued lighting.

You might ask for a copy of the obituary. The funeral home almost always has a copy they can give you. They will usually also offer you a card with the names of the deceased and immediate family members and the dates of the person's birth and death.

■ at the gravesite

More and more funeral services are taking place at the gravesite only. Sometimes this is due to the rising costs of church or funeral chapel services. Other times a simple service is performed at the gravesite because most of the family and friends are deceased or far away and there is no real need for a full-length traditional service and reception.

A simple gravesite service can be touching, dignified, and appropriate. If you have a book or binder that you use for funeral services, you will probably have to run through it and plan for a shortened version of your usual format, making some pencil markings to indicate what sections need to be shortened or eliminated.

There are a number of issues that can arise at a gravesite service, so it's best if you are prepared. There is the matter of your voice being heard outdoors by the gathered group. Not only are these groups often larger than the family anticipated, sometimes environmental factors like weather and traffic can make it difficult to be heard. The biggest unknown factor is the weather, for though it is possible that you may be at some indoor mausoleum, the odds are you will be outdoors. Funeral home people generally try to make arrangements for some kind of canopy to cover the immediate family members, a few folding chairs, and large umbrellas. Still, you will find yourself pretty exposed to the elements, whether that means rain, snow, or blinding hot sun! If you are a woman, your high-heeled shoes (yes, even the sensible ones) tend to dig themselves into the ground beneath you. Your binder with your notes in it is very often going to have its pages blowing in the wind or rained on. You won't have a place to put your bag, briefcase, purse, or the keys to your car and will likely not have sufficient pockets to accommodate all your stuff. You may also be trying to balance your binder in one hand and your Bible in the other.

Aside from this there is another discomfort that is seldom articulated by pastors but nevertheless true. Those funeral home people always show up in handsome and dignified dark suits and ties and in black or dark colored somber and expensive funeral cars. You, on the other hand, show up in your dumpy little blue two-door and wearing what always feels like the wrong clothes. After a few tries you will probably have found attire that feels right for you for these occasions. Some pastors who are accustomed to wearing an alb or robe and stole for worship services will choose the option of bringing the robe along in the car and slipping into it for the cemetery. Others choose a dignified dark suit. If the weather is cold, you will have to wear your overcoat.

■ in a family home

It is rare today for a service to be held in a family home, but it does happen. Most often, it will be a memorial service, meaning there will either be an urn with ashes present or no ashes at all. If you are asked to perform a service in a family home, be sure to go there in advance so you can see the layout, figure out with the family where you will stand when you speak, see if there is some kind of podium, determine if you will be heard without a microphone, and get an idea how many will be attending.

Sometimes a service in a house will be little more than a gathering of immediate family members to remember together the life of the loved one. You may be less an officiant and more a facilitator of conversation. You can help the family prepare for this kind of event by making the following suggestions:

* Do they have pictures to share of the person at various life stages?

* Would each person or some persons be prepared to tell a short story about the deceased?

* Do they have specific Bible passages or prayers they'd like you to offer?

* Would they like to sing some hymn or favorite song together for which you could bring copies?

■ any place you least expect

The life of a pastor, as you know, is full of surprises. A family may ask you to perform a memorial service in just about any location. Be prepared to make a pretty quick decision. If you know the people, then you will know if this location is appropriate to honor the deceased. Be sure that the closest loved one is in agreement and that this is not just the idea of one or two other family members. Sometimes the persons most bereaved are easily manipulated or find it difficult to make their wishes known. They may be deeply grief stricken and ask the family to make decisions on their behalf, but later be unhappy with the arrangements.

Ask yourself now, while you are not being rushed: "At what kind of places would I be willing to lead a service and where would I have to say no?" There is also the issue of whether and how to gracefully decline or guide the family to a better decision. You might, for example, suggest that the service be at the church and that the family can go to the mountaintop or lake they had chosen after the service, at some other time, or even on the first anniversary of the death. You can even offer to be present or help lead this later gathering in that place.

■ in another place of worship: shared leadership with another religious leader

More than once in your ministry, you will likely be asked to participate in leadership at a funeral along with another religious leader either at your church or another. At your church, the family may have requested that another pastor participate. It may be that the deceased had close family who belong to another church or even another faith, and they want their religious leader to be present and involved. Or the deceased may have been friends with this other pastor. If you are asked to invite such a person, it will be your choice whether to do so. When possible, it is good to give people what they need to help them get through those initial days of grief.

If you are invited to participate in a service at another place of worship, that religious leader will have to invite you and then guide you through the service. It will probably be good to have some kind of a run-through of the service, or at least a talk-through. The pastor at whose church the service is taking place will take the lead, and you, as the visiting pastor, will follow instructions. You can appropriately make suggestions, and you will want to be sure that whatever is decided to be your part is acceptable to you.

■ when you are asked to perform a funeral that requires travel

Someday you may be asked to officiate at a service that requires substantial travel. You may have to fly and stay overnight or even for a few days. Be sure it is understood that all your expenses are to be covered by the family. There is no reason why you should have to pay anything at all. If you know the family, you can probably have them arrange for the air tickets, hotels, and such. One caution! Be sure your ticket allows you to stay long enough for both the service and the interment.

In addition, if you are going to another state or another country, be sure to discuss with the funeral home people at the other end whether you need any special proof of your credentials as a pastor. It is best to be sure before accepting.

If you wear a robe for your Sunday services, you will probably want to bring your clergy attire along for this service. You may need to have it pressed before the service after traveling with it in your garment bag. Depending on what the family might be expecting, or on where the service will take place, robes may not be necessary. Find out ahead of time.

26

 ## officiating at the funeral of a close family member

■ a grandparent

Some people are very close to their grandparents, sometimes even raised by them. Others have a more formal or distant relationship with them. Either way, only you will know whether you are emotionally equipped to perform a service for your grandparent.

When preparing the eulogy, sermon, or both, do remember that your experience of this person, no matter how profound, represents only one aspect of the grandparent's life. Try to get information and stories about the grandparent's youth, young adulthood, and middle years. Talk to people who knew your grandparent as a friend, a sister, and of course, if possible, a spouse. My guess is that you will be very surprised. Each generation sees the person from a different angle. You will want your words at the service to reflect the whole person and not just the later years nor just your perspective as a grandchild. If you don't do this, you have not done your grandparent justice, no matter how loving your words may be.

■ a parent

It is extremely difficult to perform a funeral service for one's own parent but, for many reasons, it very often happens. Sometimes there just doesn't seem to be anyone else who is appropriate. Other times, the rest of the family expects it. You are the pastor in the family so everyone wants you to do the service. If you are pastor of a church, and your church is in keeping with your parent's denomination or theological stance, then the service might take place there. If you and your parent belong to different denominations, but your parent did not have a home church, then you might choose the funeral home.

You may not know how to begin, even if you have many funeral services under your belt. Like pastoral counseling with members of one's own family, it is just not the same. You will be in a great deal of grief. As much as you want to do your parent proud, it is very likely you will find it difficult to focus on preparing the service. In addition, memories will be pouring in, and it is difficult to sort them out to decide which might be appropriately shared in the context of the service. Aside from all this, you will be acting as both a family member and pastor to the other members of your family. If you think you can manage this, go ahead. It may mean you will have to do a good deal of your grieving at a later time. You will also miss the peace that comes from being the recipient of pastoral care and of hearing the words of consolation from another pastor. You might consider including another pastor in the service.

SCENARIO _____

> Carolyn's dad just didn't care much for pastors. It's not that he wasn't religious. He didn't hate them or anything. But there were a lot of pastors he'd met that he didn't like too much. He didn't like their asking for money. He didn't like the arrogance he felt they too often displayed. It was just a "thing" with him. Still, when he found out that his only daughter, Carolyn, was going to become a pastor, he couldn't help but be proud. Now for sure there would be one pastor he would like a lot, his darling

daughter Carolyn! So when he died, she knew for sure she would have to do the service. For one thing, her parents didn't attend church regularly. Who would they get? No, she was the one.

She realized, as she began to prepare her words, that in a way all the good things she had learned from her dad and everything she had studied in seminary had prepared her for this day. She did a lot of crying before and after the service, but she managed to lead a service that consoled her mother, that helped those present to feel the love of God, and that would have made her dad proud. Later, she wondered how she had managed. Then she remembered a Bible passage that says, "God is faithful, and he will not let you be tested beyond your strength" (1 Cor. 10:13). It was then that it came to her. All the work she had done to prepare the service, and all the busy work she'd had with being the pastor and caring for others had actually helped her to get through that difficult day. Her work as the pastor had itself been a gift to her from God. Her dad would have liked that!

■ a sibling

To officiate at the service of a sister or brother will also be very difficult, especially if you were close. Still, you have known this person for a lifetime, so who can do it better? Your work will be greatly appreciated by the family and your sibling's friends, if you are able to do it. As with the parents and grandparents, discussed above, only you will know if you have the strength to do this. If not, everyone will understand. You have every right to be on the receiving end at times like these.

■ a child or grandchild

Should the great tragedy of the loss of your own child befall you, I would guess that it would be impossible for you to lead the service, and moreover I would discourage it. You will need to be receiving the support that a worship service can bring, a service in honor and remembrance of your beloved child. You will need to cling to your spouse or other family members both in order to give and to receive consolation. If you are a seasoned pastor, and if you feel strongly that you have something you want to say, it is possible you might be able to say a few words, but leave to someone else the gift of officiating and being a pastor to you for a change.

■ a spouse

It may seem that a pastor whose beloved spouse has died could not possibly conduct or even speak at this loved one's funeral service. Still, there are some cases in which the surviving spouse feels he or she is the only one truly qualified to "say a few words." Who could know better what to say than the one who loved this person the most? There is a good chance your spouse saw you as his or her pastor. Your spouse may have expressed to you the wish that you be the one who speaks, at least the eulogy portion. When the time comes, if you are strong enough, and if you are quite convinced that it needs to be you, here are some suggestions: Prepare your words carefully. Pray for strength. And be sure you time your talk. Once you get started talking about the attributes of your loved one, you could easily go on and on. Focus on the best that the others need to hear and then let it go. It will be important, if possible, to have another pastor take charge of most of the service, maybe under your supervision but if possible not. You will need a pastor in these hard days to give you words of comfort. Allow someone to offer you that gift.

27

 relating to organizations
that honor their deceased

Some fraternal organizations perform ceremonies and rituals in honor of their members who have died. They often ask the pastor for permission or, in some cases, even expect (without asking) that they perform these ceremonies or rituals in the context of, or immediately following, the funeral service in your church. The truth is that sometimes these either clash with or repeat portions of the Christian service you are preparing. The clashing that I speak of is not something the listeners are as likely to notice as much as the pastor. This will depend, of course, on the theology of your denomination. In general, lay people tend to be much less concerned about specific theological issues than clergy. Still, you will have to be true to the theological stances of your denomination.*

As an example of the repetition problem, these ceremonies sometimes include scripture readings that you may have intended to use. If you do not know exactly what words the organization's representatives will be saying, then it is difficult for you to make your choices. You don't want the congregation at the funeral to have to be hearing two "rounds" of the same scripture. Aside from scripture, there may also be points related to death and the afterlife that are part of their ceremony. You don't want to have to change your sermon in the midst of the service.

---

*Some organizations stress the importance of works, and may also teach that works are required in order to be worthy of entering heaven. On the other hand, the Lutheran Church, for example, has a theological emphasis on "justification by faith through grace, without works of the law." For this reason, the Lutheran Church frowns upon its members' involvement in certain fraternal organizations. Other denominations that stress the importance of works may be pleased to have their members be part of such organizations.

The other obvious issue is that, between your doing your part and then the organization performing its rituals, the service can easily become far too lengthy. To be honest, there is an element of discomfort that may amount to some jealousy on the part of pastors. After all, you have been educated and prepared to be the religious leader, and these organizations' ceremonies have no shortage of theological content. Having a lay person from your community repeating rituals over a deceased member of your church can make you feel quite uncomfortable. Still, you can't really just say no, at least unless your denomination demands it. You don't want to offend family members. You don't want to act in opposition to an organization that has afforded dignity and opportunity for service to the person and that also does excellent work for the community you serve. So what are you to do?

Because the organization to which the deceased belonged is often one whose rituals are more or less secret, the leaders may not be anxious to supply you with a copy of their text. Once you have participated in one such service, you may be able to remember approximately what language and scripture they used. Still, you will have been busy performing the service so your memory may not serve you as well as usual.

If it is at all possible, it is best if you can arrange for the organization to have its rituals or ceremonies at the cemetery after you have completed yours or, even after you have left, at a different place and time than the Christian funeral. The funeral directors are likely to understand. They will usually be willing to stay at the gravesite — or other location — until the organization's ceremonies have been completed.

It is possible that you may find it really difficult to make a decision. It is, after all, very important that you maintain your theological integrity. But it is also vital that you know and respect the norms and customs of the church and the community you serve. You will want to understand and respect the things that are important to them. Many church members have been part of these organizations over a lifetime and their families have been members for generations. These organizations generally have as their goals things that are good and caring on behalf of the needy and the community. In other words, their goals are much like those of the church and they also teach their members, as Jesus taught, to love others above self. If you need help in decision making, you can perhaps speak with the former pastor, or chat with leaders in your church and community, and then give the matter your prayerful consideration. It's best to think through some of these issues before they arise — because they will.

part four

funeral sermons

28

 sermon samples and ideas

The sermons in this chapter are not intended to be used by the reader in any "fill in the blank" sense. Every death, as every life, is unique and every service of remembrance requires its own set of words. In addition, every pastor has a style. Nor are these sermons intended to be models, but rather examples of the sermons that one pastor might write to offer hope and consolation. These sermons probably contain words, phrases, or theologies that you would not choose. In other cases, the words may ring true to your style and can offer some jumping off points for your own funeral sermons.

The need to produce a funeral sermon so often comes in our busiest times. We want so much to offer the best we have to the bereaved families. I hope that these sermons will give you some ideas that you can adapt when needed. (All the names and situations are, of course, fictitious.)

■ funeral sermon for an elderly person, lifting up the person's faithfulness to his or her church, work, family

Well done, good and faithful servant. (Matt. 25:21 KJV)

Dear Friends,

Today we have come together in this holy place to say farewell to Jean-Ann Randolph. We are here to say goodbye to a woman who has led a good life, and especially to celebrate that faithful life. Jean-Ann was predeceased by her beloved husband of thirty-eight years, George, and is survived by her daughter, Grace Boxford, and husband, Robert, and their children — Mary, Martin, and Linda-Ann. She is also survived by one brother, Frank Soames of New York City, and one sister, Mary-Rose Linton of Jupiter, Florida.

Jean-Ann also had many good and loyal friends. You, her dear friends, are here today, surrounding the family with your love and caring support. Jean-Ann would have liked that. As you all know, she was always there for all of us.

The words of the parable at Matthew 25:21 "Well done, good and faithful servant" are commonly read at funeral services. But they are especially appropriate in remembering Jean-Ann. From all we know of her, we might expect these will also be the words she will hear when she arrives in that heavenly home.

Jean-Ann was both good and faithful in so many ways. She was good and faithful in caring for her mother during the long years of her illnesses. She was good and faithful, working so hard all those years alongside her beloved husband, George, in their bookstore — building up the business to such a success. She was good and faithful in her many years of community service, with the Girl Scouts, as president of the women's music guild, and of course here at the church. And she served on so many committees here. She baked thousands of cookies, which all of us have enjoyed. She was always there in the Sunday School when she was needed.

We depended on Jean-Ann. We depended on her goodness — her kind and tender heart. And we depended on her faithfulness.

We could always trust her to come through for her family, for her community, and for us. Jean-Ann was truly God's good and faithful servant.

What would she want now? She'd want us to carry on. And she'd hope that we too would be good and faithful servants of Jesus Christ. We will miss her dearly — but we will go on. When we carry on her work at the church, we will be honoring her memory.

And Jean-Ann has gone on to a better place. We don't know the details about the experience after death we call heaven. All we have are a few glimpses "through a glass darkly," as Paul says. But we have God's promises. Each of us will die someday, but we are the people of the promise. When it comes to the future, God calls us to trust. When it comes to the present, God calls us to be good and faithful servants. This is exactly what Jean-Ann personified. Today we celebrate this life well lived, we live in God's eternal promises, and we say goodbye to her in hope and trust.

Let us pray.

Gracious God, it is you who created us. It is you who sustains us through life and death and life beyond death. We thank you today for your unending love. We thank you especially for the life of Jean-Ann and for all she has meant to us. We ask, O Holy One, that you lift up and watch over all the family and all who loved her so much as they go through this most difficult time of grieving. Help us to continue lives of love and service here on earth until at your chosen time you take us to be with you forever. We thank you for it all in the name of Jesus, the Christ. Amen.

■ funeral sermon for a highly accomplished person

We gather here this afternoon to mourn the death and to celebrate the life of Conrad Burlay. We are here to mourn this man who was a good husband to his beloved Leah, a loving father to Marcy and Granger, a devoted brother to Charles, a colleague to so many of you here today, and a friend to all. Today we celebrate a life of honor, of responsibility, of great accomplishment, of service, and an example to others. Conrad was truly an exceptional man.

We are here to mourn today, to mourn and remember. But we will also hear the words of hope and consolation. We will hear the promises of Christ that life is even more than meets the eye, and that we belong to God not only for life but for life eternal.

Let us pray.

O God of grace and mercy, God of love and restoration, we remember before you today the life of your servant, Conrad Burlay. We thank you for his presence among us in the lives of those here gathered, and for giving Conrad to us to know and to love. In your boundless and unending compassion, console those who mourn. Help us to see, in death, the doorway to life eternal. Be with us and give us strength for the days and years ahead. We ask this in the name of Jesus Christ. Amen.

Hear the words of scripture from Psalm 27, verses 1 and 14.

The Lord is my light and my salvation; whom shall I fear?
The Lord is the stronghold of my life; of whom shall I be
    afraid? . . .
Wait for the Lord; be strong, and let your heart take
    courage;
Wait for the Lord!

Conrad Burlay has been described recently by our mayor, Henry Martin, as "a man who never stopped giving." Just last year he was named in the *American Business Journal* as "generous to a fault, wise and witty." He was a man of great accomplishment. These are great things without a doubt. But Conrad was more than that. A lot of people accomplish a lot of good things and then they go their way. He was different. Conrad knew how to turn to the people who had made it possible for him to do all the great good he did and to thank them and to help them. He gave back to those who had been a part of his successes. He never forgot the people along the way. That is a big part of his greatness.

It is probably known by all of you here that Conrad always made an exceptional effort on behalf of others, not just an effort but an exceptional effort. The organizations he supported on behalf of justice and for those in need constitute a long list. But it was not just his financial support that these organizations could count on. He also gave personal support with his time and his talents.

Conrad is at rest now, after a long and debilitating illness. He is at rest after a lifetime commitment to people. You who remember him will carry with you, all of your lives, not only his great example but also your memories of all he has meant to you. He was a person of character and commitment to his values. He was, in the end, what could be called the most mature kind of Christian: one who lived for others. Jesus talked continually about something called the Reign of God, a time or a place where we do not live for self but for others. Conrad was a role model for us all.

And we are called to continue, during our lives on this earth, also committed to the building of that Reign of God. We will remember Conrad and his life and his gift of service.

So now in the sure and certain hope of the resurrection to eternal life through our Lord Jesus Christ, we commit to Almighty God our brother Conrad Burlay.

■ funeral sermon for a child

THEOLOGICAL REFLECTION

Weeping may linger for the night, but joy comes in the morning. (Psalm 30:5b)

Life, as we all know, has its ups and downs, sometimes very big ones. The psalm, Psalm 30, in a later verse (verse 11) comments that "you have turned my mourning into dancing." Some events in life are deeply devastating and one would feel that surely there will never again be any joy or dancing. Yet, God's promise here is clear. There will be healing and even joy again, no matter what suffering life may have brought. This is the hope in which we live and which makes it possible for us to get through the times of deepest suffering.

The death of a baby, child, or young person seems so senseless. God stands by us in all things, the good and the very bad. We are not alone. We live in the promises of God.

The sermon that follows is an example of a sermon at the death of a child, in this case a child who had died very shortly after being born. Like the other sermons, it is offered only as an example. The situation and of course the names are fictional.

Dearly Beloved,

We are gathered here today to lay to rest Jacob Ricky Simms, son of Mary and Richard Harry Simms. God is with us in this place as we remember little Jacob. God knows your sorrow that is deeper than words can express.

Let us pray.

O God, we know that you would not ever have one of your precious children hurt in any way. You would never choose that a child should die or that parents be left feeling that they are without hope.

Though the world can bring pain, we trust you to sustain us through it all.

It is difficult to thank you, God, in a time of such sadness. Still, we acknowledge the gift of life that you have given to each one of us. We are grateful for the love that is present here today among the family and friends, as we support this young couple through their time of loss.

We know that you sustain this family today, holding them tenderly in your arms of love. Even if at this time they may not be able to see a future beyond their tears, guide them and help them to know that in some way and in time their sorrow will be eased. Trusting in your loving care, we pray in the name of Jesus Christ, Amen.

Today we sadly gather to say goodbye to little Jacob. No one knows how to do that. When we hold a service for someone who has lived a full and long life, the feelings are quite different. The tears are different today. We don't know who little Jacob was going to be. His life will remain a mystery, a kind of dream in the minds of all of us. You had been waiting for his arrival with so much hope and excitement. Your dream of him will not be the same as what his life here would have been, because that no one can know. He missed his life on earth except for a few short days. He missed the joys of sunshine, of rain on his face, of school and of work, of marriage and of raising his own family. He also missed the inevitable disappointments and the suffering that life brings.

In our thoughts, Jacob will always be perfect too. He didn't make any mistakes, because he didn't have the chance for that either. Making those mistakes is a real part of living.

It must be so hard for you, Mary and Richard. Though everyone means to console you, no one can know how you feel.

I am here as your pastor to give words of comfort when no comfort seems possible. Still, take what I say today, along with the love from all these dear friends gathered here, and hold it in your hearts for later. As time passes, although you will always love and miss Jacob, your pain will begin to ease just a bit, and then some more.

So these are the words I offer to you today. Our God is a God of Love. God never hurts people. Being alive and free and in a world that works by the rules of nature means that things go wrong sometimes, and that's what happened. But God has never left your side. God has suffered with you. God understands the death of a son.

Your little Jacob is safe now in the arms of Jesus. Remember, Jesus loved children and children flocked to his side. He took the little children on his knee, and blessed them and said to his disciples, "Let the children come to me, and do not stop them; for it is to such as these that the kingdom of heaven belongs" (Matt. 19:14).

You are grieving now. Grieving has different stages and no two people grieve the same way at the same time. You will each grieve for this dear child in your own way and in your own time. Be very good to each other, Mary and Richard, and try to understand the pain the other is in.

Your precious Jacob did not have to suffer. He did not have to go through so much of human living: the disappointments and the pain. And he is safe now with God in a good place and in a way that none of us who are living can know.

You who longed so much to know him, to care for him, love him, and watch him grow — you will go on, because you have to go on. You won't be the same, but you will be okay. God will help you. There is a Bible passage that I hope will help you. Here is what the Apostle Paul said:

I am convinced that neither death, nor life,
nor angels, nor rulers,
nor things present, nor things to come,
nor powers, nor height, nor depth,
nor anything else in all creation,
will be able to separate us from the love of God in Christ
    Jesus our Lord. (Rom. 8:38–39)

So, dear ones, know this. Nothing can separate your Jacob from the love of God, and nothing can separate you from God's love either.

Let us pray.

Loving God, we know you have welcomed this little child,
Jacob Ricky Simms, into your keeping, into your arms of
love. Keep his precious family who waits on this shore of
life in your care. May they be surrounded by your angels.
Bless all who mourn here today. Fill us with hope and trust
in your promises. Stay close beside us always. We ask this
in the name of Jesus Christ. Amen.

part five

funeral resources at your church

29

 benefits and potential problems of a memorial garden

■ purpose of the garden

A memorial garden on your church property can serve as an incentive to attract people to your church and also to keep members close to the church, for a number of reasons. Often bereaved people will tell the pastor: "I just can't drag myself to church anymore. Every time I step into the sanctuary, I remember how happy we were together here, and I can't stop crying." If their loved one is buried in another location, they may stop coming to church. If the ashes have been placed in your memorial garden on the church's property, the bereaved may feel closer to the loved one. They may even experience some sense of obligation to attend and support the church, and continue on as part of the faith community. This may sound a bit coercive on the part of the church. It is good for the church, but also for the bereaved, who are encouraged to remain within the circle of love that the church has to offer.

Memorial gardens also offer a practical and cost-effective alternative to cemeteries. For this reason, they sometimes attract older people to churches. Older people are then able to make advance plans, resting assured that at least in this respect their passing will not financially burden their children.

■ getting a garden started

As a pastor, you may have come to serve a church that already has a memorial garden. Whether you have a memorial garden when you begin your ministry in a particular church or have had any thoughts at all about starting one, you should find this section useful.

Memorial gardens differ and churches have their own ways, so there is plenty of room for creativity on your part. The most common way that pastors and committees decide how to organize their new memorial garden is by learning from neighboring churches that have successfully created and are maintaining theirs.

■ types of memorial gardens

Memorial gardens vary widely, from the way they look to the way they are operated. Often their physical look is related to their location. A church with a large stone edifice in the center of a busy city may have a smaller space allocated for the garden with, perhaps, a large bronze plaque on which the names of the deceased are engraved. The flowers and plants that grow there may be fewer and adaptable to the environment of the inner city.

Such a garden might be enclosed within a stone or brick wall for privacy and may have a stone or marble bench for loved ones to sit on when they come to visit.

In the case of a church that is more suburban or rural, the memorial garden can be any size, sometimes encompassing a large portion of the church property. Some memorial gardens will allow some sort of small marker for each name to be placed where the ashes have been poured or scattered. Other gardens only have a large rock in some carefully chosen spot in the garden onto which small brass plates are attached, each with the name of a deceased person whose ashes are somewhere in the garden. Some memorial gardens have many trees and shrubs that require minimum care. Others will be filled with flowering plants that change with the seasons, a garden in which continuous plant-ings and prunings are required. The gardeners are nearly always church members, so keep this in mind if you and your committee are making a master plan.

What will the space look like? Some gardens begin around a tree (often an older beautiful, strong tree). This facilitates a clockwise circular plan with ashes being placed at the various points, just as each five minutes are apart on a clock, and then in ever widening circles moving outward from the first circle around the tree. The church keeps a chart that the family can consult to locate the exact spot where their loved one's ashes have been placed. This way, there is no need for the names to be engraved on markers at the actual location.

It is better if you can avoid having ashes placed in a specific spot that has to be recorded and remembered. The reason for this is that, if you don't have specific locations for each person, you can use the garden into the future without running out of space. But then what are family members to do when they return a week or a month later to visit the place where the ashes have been deposited? Here is one option. A small wooden cross, about one or two feet high, with a sharp pointed end, can be inserted into the ground directly above the spot where the ashes have been placed. This little cross should be left in that location for thirty to sixty days (or somewhat longer if weather is not an issue) and then removed to be used again. This way, during that early period, the loved ones can return and easily find the location. At the outset you will also have explained to them that the entire garden is a memorial to their dear one, as it is also for the others, so there is no need to permanently record the location where particular ashes are placed.

Often a family will purchase a brass plaque in memory of their loved one and have it engraved with their name and the person's birth and death dates. The plaque will be placed along with the others on a large rock in the garden, as mentioned earlier. The rock may be positioned in a beautiful grove, beside a particularly fine tree, or near benches. Brass plaques do not come cheap, so arrangements to place ashes in the garden should also include the family's agreement to pay the cost of its purchase of the plaque.

If the person was a church member, it may also be a tradition of your church to have a plaque inside the church building with the names of those members who have died. Those whose ashes are in the garden are not always only church members. You will need to make rules regarding who may be included: family of church members, or even other non-members. This will make things easier for you as the pastor whenever families ask.

■ laws related to memorial gardens

Cities and towns are concerned about any space set aside for burial of the dead. This is at least partly because, in the years that follow your decision for a memorial garden, this "holy ground" usually can no longer be designated for any other purpose. For this reason, your decision to start a memorial garden will nearly always have to be approved by some local government. So before you go deeply into decision making about the start up of a memorial garden, be sure to check the laws and regulations of your city, town, or county. In many cases, laws state that once a part of a package of land has been designated for a memorial garden, then the whole property can never be resold for any reason. You may think this is a non-issue right now for your church, but nobody knows what the future will bring.

SCENARIO _____

Pastor Bob served a church in California that had been built twenty years earlier on a piece of land that looked as if it would always be relatively rural and quiet. By the time Bob arrived, the street where the church was located was getting a fair amount of traffic. Still, nobody expected a housing boom! The congregation had started a memorial garden in a small circle spreading out around a big beautiful oak tree. They anticipated four to six circles of "sites" for ashes, moving outward, all around that tree. As it turned out, because the congregation consisted mainly of seniors, in the twenty years of the church's existence, they had already filled up seven circles. As a result, the memorial garden was inching closer and closer to the main road. At the same time, the street on which the church stood was becoming more and more valuable for business use. The city was also growing like wildfire on the other side of town. It became obvious that the best strategy for Bob's church would have been to sell the church buildings and property and build for growth on the other side of town. This, however, was not an option any more. The reason was simple. The memorial garden had been officially deemed a cemetery by the city, and the property could no longer be sold—ever. A sister church of the same denomination ended up building a big church on the other side of town and it filled up with young families almost immediately. Pastor Bob's church, thanks to that memorial garden, continued to struggle along just to stay alive. Still, the members felt consoled, knowing they were serving God and each other in their particular way.

■ opportunities for members to participate

No matter how small your church or its memorial garden, you will need the approval of your church boards as well as real support of an active memorial garden committee. The committee will have numerous responsibilities, including:

Planning and facilitating the smooth operation of the garden

The memorial garden committee, under your guidance, will oversee the creation and maintenance of the garden. They will look ahead in order to avoid future problems. They will oversee all subcommittees or individuals with specific jobs related to the garden. They may raise monies to cover expenses and will also be the ones to purchase any outdoor furniture such as benches where family and friends may sit and rest when visiting the garden.

Planting and caring for flowers and plants and keeping the property in excellent condition

An attractive looking garden is important for the sake of the families of the deceased, for church members, and even for any residences and business establishments in the immediate area. It is easier to get a memorial garden started than to maintain one over many years. Unless the church can afford a professional gardener, it takes an ongoing group of church members with dedication and green thumbs!

Collecting any fees related to the placement of ashes in the memorial garden

Memorial garden fee collection will likely be a new part of the job description for your stewardship and finance committee. Generally, church committees like to do things the way they always have in the past, so they may not be too anxious to take on this additional responsibility. It may be possible for a new subcommittee or an individual member of the finance committee to take on this job. Mainly they will receive fees for initial placement in the garden to cover such things as the cost of a brass plaque. The memorial garden committee will have planned the running of the garden in such a way that the larger expenses are covered by donated memorial monies.

Purchasing and placing memorial plaques

It will likely be the responsibility of another group or individual to gather the information about the deceased and then purchase and place a memorial plaque on a rock or wall each time ashes are added to the garden (if you have this system.) As mentioned earlier, most often it is better if the plaque is not put in the actual location where the ashes have been placed. Ideally these are placed within a month or two of the death, or at least in the first year. Brass is best as it can withstand the weather over many years and maintain its beauty and the clarity of the engraved words.

Keeping the memorial garden records

Some bookkeeping person or subcommittee needs to be responsible for maintaining a very clear and accurate record of the full name of the deceased, the exact date of birth, death, and date of the placement of the ashes in the garden, and, if applicable, the exact location. Keep in mind that many years can pass and suddenly a family member may appear and request information. Both you and the pastors who follow you will be grateful for well-maintained records. It is important that the records be kept in the church building and not at a member's home. Even long-time members move away or leave the church. They also could die and have family members who discard these precious records before you have a chance to pick them up. It is a good policy for the pastor and church leaders to keep all important records safely stored on church property with a record of their location in a prominent place in the pastor's office.

Assisting the pastor in placing of the ashes

The job of assisting the pastor is often taken on by deacons or elders of the church. It involves such practical and important matters as helping the pastor to remove the ashes (usually in a large plastic bag) from their outer box and then from the (usually plastic) container. You may be able to do this yourself. Still, with all that's going on, you will appreciate help, as the plastic containers do not open easily. This elder or deacon can then carry the ashes out to the garden. You may carry them yourself, of course, but your hands will already be full, carrying your notes, a Bible or Psalm book, and possibly even an umbrella, gloves, or other items. Once you get to the garden, this person can assist you. He or she may lift any cover over the hole, which has been dug in advance, help you pour the ashes, hold an umbrella over you if it's raining, or even be available to console family members. On occasion such a person has even offered to take photographs of the gathered family.

Writing articles in the church newsletter

This job needs good writers. Articles can offer both information and news about the garden. They might include such matters as information about new plantings, times or seasons when the garden will be particularly beautiful to visit, an invitation to the garden as a place for quiet meditation, thank-you notes for donations for the garden, and, of course, the names of any whose ashes have been most recently placed there. This person or committee will also update and distribute any brochures related to the memorial garden. A monthly newsletter article will keep church members aware of the garden, its importance to the church, and any needs related to its improvement and maintenance.

30

 preparing a resource
booklet on death and dying
with church members

THEOLOGICAL REFLECTION _____

When this perishable body puts on imperishability, and this mortal body puts on immortality, then the saying that is written will be fulfilled, "Death has been swallowed up in victory." Where, O Death, is your victory? Where, O Death, is your sting? The sting of death is sin, and the power of sin is the law. But thanks be to God who gives us the victory through our Lord Jesus Christ. (1 Cor. 15:54–57)

It is the hope and expectation of all Christians that death will end in victory. This glorious passage from Paul's first letter to the Corinthians tells us that, because of Jesus Christ, sin no longer has power over us and we are safe with God when the time comes to die. It is human to fear that death will be the end. This passage strongly refutes the finality of death, and can offer consolation and hope to those who are bereaved.*

_____

*For this section on the preparation of a booklet for church members on death and dying, I am especially grateful to the following:

The late Rev. Theodore C. Schoonover, who passed away in March 2003. He was minister of Avon Congregational Church (UCC) in Avon, Connecticut, for sixteen years, retiring in the 1980s, and then minister emeritus. It was his idea for that church to prepare such a booklet.

The members of the Death and Dying Booklet Committee of St. Andrew United Church of Christ in Sarasota, Florida, where I served as pastor for five years. Committee members: church members Fay Donaldson (then, church president), Charles Boaz, the Rev. John Borresen, Margaret Durham, the Rev. Jake Jacobs, Ted Leed, and Violet Zehr (parish nurse).

■ why a booklet on death and dying?

Creating a resource booklet for church members related to issues of death and dying may seem a negative action at first, yet such a booklet can be a very welcome help. Those who read and use such booklets say they become better prepared and more comfortable about dealing with matters connected with what will be the last years (or months or days) of their lives. Such booklets are especially appropriate for congregations with large numbers of seniors, although they are good for any congregation since we engage in little open conversation about death and dying. We tend to want to forget that death is in every person's future including our own. We seem to avoid the topic of death at all costs, at least until a death is upon us or those we love.

Still we worry, often in silence, about how we will handle the end of our lives. Who will arrange for our funeral service? What will our obituary say about us? How will our precious belongings be distributed? Where will we be buried?

Many of us are unwilling to attend workshops or other gatherings where these matters are spoken about. For these reasons, people are often grateful for a booklet that helps them think through a variety of death-related issues, a booklet that helps them make some preliminary plans and good advance decisions. Christians can get ready for death and can do it well when the time comes. Confronting death realistically, and preparing emotionally, spiritually, and practically can bring your church members much consolation. The booklet can also facilitate open communications with the people they love. It can help us stop behaving as if we're going to live on this earth forever and begin to accept the reality of death.

■ working with a team or committee

It is best if you can gather a team or committee from among your church members (those who have an interest in the issue) and prepare the booklet together over a period of a few weeks or months. This way, the committee members will have a special sense of ownership. Their participation may also make the booklet more appealing to the rest of the church members. The more input they have, the better the booklet will be.

■ topics to cover

- Decisions about accepting death and planning for events related to the time of death
- Decisions about disposal of possessions — not just the major financial issues but also any smaller gifts the person might want to bequeath. For example, gifts such as jewelry, china, or a collection of stamps or coins might be appreciated by some particular person. There is no real reason why the actual giving needs to wait until the person has died.
- Decisions about death with dignity
- Decisions about the disposal of the body
- Decisions about donating organs or tissues for transplant, or the body for research
- Decisions about endowment gifts to the church or other organizations
- Decisions about location for the funeral or memorial service
- Decisions about who will officiate
- Decisions about whether to display the body (at the visitation, service, or both)
- Decisions about the preference for burial or cremation
- Decisions about flowers or memorial gifts
- General information about funeral directors and memorial societies in the area

■ checklists to include

A good booklet to help people with matters of death and dying will ideally include a couple of checklists that church members can fill out on their own time. One will list items that they have to take care of by themselves. A second list is to be left in a prearranged location for the family to consult after the death. It will give direction to those loved ones who will have to look after matters after death occurs. It will include:

- The person's choices of what to do when death occurs (within legal boundaries, of course)

- Details about the service, all those who need to be notified and their phone numbers

- Personal matters, household issues, and business issues.

- Addresses, emails, and telephone numbers of the following:

  - the person's attorney, executor, employer or employees, insurance company or agent

  - Social Security Administration, Veterans Administration (if the person is a veteran), landlord or mortgage company. It might also include a list of friends and family who should be notified

- The location of insurance policies, real estate deeds or mortgages, pension records, birth certificate, marriage certificate, stocks and bonds, bank books, automobile titles, and the deed to any cemetery plot owned.

- Advice about what information should be included in an obituary. It may seem morbid to write one's own obituary in advance, but there is often no one person, even a family member, who knows all the details of one's life and accomplishments. If a person does not want to write a personal obituary, then a list of important dates, family members' names, work life, accomplishments, and pertinent life events will help greatly.

- Information related to the process of giving endowment bequests or gift annuities to the church. Such gifts can be set up well in advance of a person's death. In many cases, the person can enjoy the giving while also receiving, during the lifetime, the interest income from the gift annuity. In addition, often up to one-third of the gift may be tax deductible and one third of the annuity also income tax free. A classic situation of "everybody wins!" Older people or those in ill health often want to make this kind of gift and do not know how to proceed. You should include information in a separate section, telling exactly what steps they can take to make such a gift. (For example, they might contact the chairperson or a member of the stewardship committee or financial board.) Be very careful to check with professional financial advisors so you get your facts straight in this section of the booklet.

- A bibliography of useful books or DVDs related to issues of death and dying, as well as addresses, phone numbers, and good websites where people can get more information. If possible include a separate sheet listing any upcoming lectures, classes, or workshops in your area on topics related to death and dying. In addition it would be especially practical if you earmark those books in the bibliography that are currently available in your church library.

- Other death-related topics that could be included in the booklet are dying with dignity, explaining death to children, Hospice and how it works, donating organs or tissues for transplant, and decisions about donating one's body for medical educational purposes.

■ choosing a good title for the booklet

There are many possibilities for good titles for the booklet your church produces. You might ask your committee to submit ideas for the title and then vote on them. It is possible also to get the entire congregation involved by helping to choose a title. Remember, the more they're involved in producing the booklet, the more they are likely to appreciate, use, and promote it.

conclusion

We've moved together through the many issues related to meeting the needs of today's families at the time of a death. We've walked together from the first phone call to the service itself, then to the cemetery and the reception. We've thought through ideas for funeral sermons. We've considered special circumstances. And we've finished up with two important things you can do for your church: setting up a memorial garden, and preparing a booklet on death and dying for your church members. You are ready now to handle all funeral-related issues. In addition, you are even prepared to lead your church members to a willingness to face the fact that all of us will die. As Jesus says, "Keep awake therefore, for you do not know on what day your Lord is coming.... Therefore, you must be ready, for the Son of Man is coming at an unexpected hour" (Matt. 24:42, 44). You and your congregations, at least in a practical sense, will have taken some small steps in being "ready."

appendix: recommended scripture readings

Old Testament

Job 19:25–27a: "I know that my Redeemer lives."

Psalm 23: "The Lord is my shepherd, I shall not want."

Psalm 27:1, 4–9a, 13–14: "The Lord is my light and my salvation."

Psalm 42:1–7: "As a deer longs for flowing streams, so my soul longs for you, O God."

Psalm 46:1–7: "God is our refuge and strength, a very present help in trouble."

Psalm 90: "Lord, you have been our dwelling place in all generations."

Psalm 106:1–5: "Praise the Lord! O give thanks to the Lord, for he is good."

Psalm 121: "I lift up my eyes to the hills — from where will my help come?"

Psalm 130: "Out of the depths I cry to you, O Lord. Lord, hear my voice."

Psalm 139: "O Lord, you have searched me and known me."

Psalm 143: "Hear my prayer, O Lord; give ear to my supplications."

Isaiah 25:7b–9: "He [God] will swallow up death forever."

Isaiah 40:28–31: "Those who wait for the Lord shall renew their strength."

Lamentations 3:22–26, 31–33: "The steadfast love of the Lord never ceases."

New Testament

Matthew 5:1–12a: "Rejoice and be glad, for your reward is great in heaven."

Matthew 11:25–30: "Come to me . . . and I will give you rest."

Luke 7:11–17: Jesus raises the son of the widow.

Luke 12:35–40: Be prepared.

Luke 23:33, 39–43: "Today you will be with me in Paradise."

John 3:16–21: "God so loved the world."

John 6:37–40: "Everything that the Father gives me will come to me."

John 6:51–59: "Whoever eats of this bread will live forever."

John 11:21–27: "I am the resurrection and the life."

John 12:23–28: "Unless a grain of wheat falls into the earth and dies."

John 14:1–6: "In my Father's house there are many dwelling places."

Romans 5:1–11: "Justified by faith, we have peace with God."

Romans 6:3–9: "So that we too might walk in newness of life."

1 Corinthians 15:20–26, 35–38, 42–44, 50, 53–58: "Death has been swallowed up in victory."

2 Corinthians 4:16–5:1: "What can be seen is temporary, but what cannot be seen is eternal."

2 Corinthians 5:1, 6–10: We have an everlasting home in heaven.

Philippians 3:20–21: "But our citizenship is in heaven."

1 Thessalonians 4:13–18: "So we will be with the Lord forever."

2 Timothy 2:8–13: "If we have died with him, we also will live with him."

1 John 3:1–9: "We will see him as he is."

Revelation 7:9–17: "God will wipe away every tear from their eyes."

Revelation 14:1–3, 6–7, 12–13: Rest for the saints.

Revelation 21:2–7: A new heaven and a new earth.

For the death of a child

Lamentations 3:1–9, 19–23: God's steadfast love.

Matthew 18:1–5, 10: Greatest in the kingdom of heaven.

Mark 10:13–16: "Let the children come to me."

1 John 3:1–3: We are children of God.

scripture index

general index

Accidental death, 80
Booklet on issues of death and dying, 124–27
Bulletins, 38
Caskets, purchase of, 16
Cemetery plot, 19–21
Challenged people at the service, 89–90
  hearing challenged, 89
  mentally challenged, 90
  physically challenged, 90
  sight challenged, 90
Children of the deceased, 76, 87, 92
Children who have died, 25, 27, 78, 111–14, 131
Coffins. *See* caskets
Communion, 56
Cortege, Funeral, 62
Cost of funerals, 10, 12
Done wrong, funerals for those who have, 92–94
Elderly, services for, 75
Eulogy, 39, 55
Ex-spouses of the deceased, 29–30, 91–92
Exits from sanctuary or chapel, 61

Family, meeting with, 7–8
Family participation in service, 37–42
Family member, officiating at a funeral of
  children, 101–2
  grandchildren, 101–2
  grandparents, 99
  parents, 100
  siblings, 101
  spouse, 102
Fees for funeral. *See* cost of funerals
Fees for memorial garden, 120
Flowers, 10, 44–45, 116, 126
Gay and Lesbian persons, funerals of, 33–34, 69–71
Gravesite services, 17, 63–66, 95–96
Guestbook, 44
Home, funerals in a family, 96
Illness, death after a lifelong, 81–82
Memorial garden on church property, 64–66, 115–23
Military, funerals for, 84–87